Did You Know That...

• All books are not equal? Carefully chosen literature can help your child progress from one developmental stage to the next.

• There are special ''flap'' books to stimulate your child's natural wonder and delight in secrets?

• The time to buy textured books is between six months and one year, when your baby delights in touching and stroking?

• 18 to 24 months is the age to introduce alphabet books as your baby's repertoire of abilities and experiments grows?

• You should wait until 18 months to give pop-up books or they will be torn apart?

• Between two and three your toddler is likely to be more fascinated by books with photographs than by those with illustrations?

For every stage there are special books. Here's the indispensable guide that tells you how to recognize and where to buy the best books to inspire your child with a love of learning that will last a lifetime.

GOOD BOOKS TO GROW ON

A GUIDE TO BUILDING YOUR CHILD'S LIBRARY FROM BIRTH TO AGE FIVE

Andrea E. Cascardi

WARNER BOOKS

A Warner Communications Company

A Warner Communications Company

Printed in the United States of America
First Printing: October 1985
10 9 8 7 6 5 4 3 2 1

Library of Congress Cataloging in Publication Data

Cascardi, Andrea E.
  Good books to grow on.

  Includes index.
  1. Children's literature—Bibliography.
  2. Bibliography—Best books—Children's literature.
  3. Picture books for children—Bibliography.
  4. Children—Books and reading. I. Title.
Z1037.C353 1985 [PN1009.A1] 011'.6250543 85-7114
ISBN 0-446-38173-X (U.S.A.)(pbk.)
   0-446-38174-8 (Canada)(pbk.)

Designed by Giorgetta Bell McRee

Contents

Acknowledgments

I would like to thank the following people, who provided me with lists of recommended books for preschoolers and contributed personal anecdotes or general information about their experience with pre-readers and books:

Amy Cohn, _The Horn Book_

Laurel June Burr, formerly of the Harvard Bookstore Cafe, Boston, Massachusetts

Mary Lee Donovan, formerly of The Children's Bookshop, Brookline, Massachusetts

Ellen Fader, Westport Library, Connecticut

Ruth Roland and Peggy Byrd, consultants in children's literature and parent education, the Open Door Bookshop, Greensboro, North Carolina

Judith F. Davie, Department of Library Science and Educational Technology, University of North Carolina at Greensboro

Sher Smith, the Secret Garden Bookshop, Seattle, Washington

Andrea and Steven Ozment, Newbury, Massachusetts

Hannah Scheffler, Early Childhood Resources Center, Leroy Street Library (New York Public Library), Manhattan

Marcia Wattson, B. Dalton Booksellers, Minneapolis, Minnesota, for catalogue information.

The following organizations provided me with their lists of recommended books for young children:

National Association for the Education of Young Children
Children's Book Council
Child Study Association, Children's Book Committee
American Library Association, Preschool Services and Parent Education Committee of the Association for Library Service to Children
The New York Public Library

In addition, I would like to thank the Davis family: Ken, Joann, and Jenny, who are responsible for the idea from which this book grew.

Preface

ENCOURAGING BOOK READING

$\mathcal{I}$ have very strong memories of encouraging my children to read. But the single clearest memory I have is paying my son (a Montessori school graduate) a penny a page to read when he was in first grade. Each page, each book, was an effort for him. Oh, he would read—and very well, at that—but only what was required. Beyond that, forget it . . . and I have. Life has its compensations, though; his sister reads enough extra books for both of them.

Your child may never develop enthusiasm for reading. It isn't something you can force, and it may happen after you've given up all hope. (I'm still hoping . . . as I bite my lip, thinking that my son, who's now doing very well in high school, may never get interested in anything more literary than Garfield collections.) I'm still trying to give it my best shot, though. A love of books and reading is something to be nurtured. I said you can't force it, but you can certainly *encourage* it.

Perhaps the single most important thing that you can do is to start early. Making books a part of your infant's environment from the day you bring him or her home from the hospital will mean that books are fixed in the child's mind as a part of life—as significant to him as the toys, mobiles, dolls, and pictures he will come to cherish. Nowadays, there are wonderful books for the very youngest of children—books to hang over cribs, soft books that can go right into the crib, plastic books for the tub. They will help your child explore his new world. They entertain, they stimulate, they excite, they educate. And the impressions that these books can create in children will last a lifetime. You will see this as you read through this book and perhaps rediscover some of your own childhood favorites, like *Madeline* or *Make Way for Ducklings*. They are books that will bring a smile to your face as you say to yourself, "I remember that!"

Here are some other tips for creating the reading habit:

• First, by your own example. "Do as I say, not as I do" just doesn't apply here.

• By reading aloud. If bedtime doesn't work for you, it can be a nice family tradition over breakfast.

• By letting a restless child, who has trouble simply listening, doodle or draw while you read.

• By making it a family tradition to give a special book annually for certain holidays.

• By reading to your children even when they're old enough to read themselves. If you have a fireplace to read around, do it! If only one child will listen, read to that child; the others will often drift in. Make reading aloud a round-robin family affair.

Libraries and bookstores in our country are two of our most prized reading resources. I think we must rival other countries with the variety and accessibility that both of these offer. They are designed to invite us in to browse and participate. Encourage your children to take advantage of all the library has to offer:

• Have your children sign up for library cards as soon as they are old enough. I think mine were in kindergarten at the time. It was (*is*) a big deal and they feel *so* grown up.

• Help your kids pick out books, especially when they're very little, but let them select some of their own, too, even if they don't seem particularly appropriate to you.

• Take your preschooler to story hours and other such library activities, and don't overlook the possibilities for older children, too. Some libraries have films, records, tapes, and special programs, including computer education, for older kids.

• Help your child become acquainted with the librarian, that person who's always ready, willing, and able to find special books and answer questions.

Browse the bookstores, too. Store managers can help when you are in doubt about what is age-appropriate.

Some more thoughts on children and books:

Don't make judgments about your children's choice of books. Never make reading a punishment. Older children need to revert to "baby" books at times. If a book is beyond your child's reading level, but is of interest because of the subject matter, don't be discouraging. It's not necessary that every word or thought be understood perfectly. Fantasy, mystery, even romances offer something special to the world of imagination.

> **Vicki Lansky,**
> author of
> *Feed Me I'm Yours* and
> *Practical Parenting Tips,*
> and many other publications
> for parents of young children

GOOD
BOOKS
═══ TO ═══
GROW ON

Introduction

*T*he reason for this book begins with the notion that putting books and babies together is not simply an interesting idea or a wild-eyed experiment. We know that babies need books just as they need songs and laughter and toys and games and affection: to encourage and stimulate their motor, social, emotional, and intellectual development.

Publishers, teachers, and librarians have responded to that thinking, encouraged by the considerable research of experts in the child development field. Years ago publishers began producing books for the very youngest of children, surprising many adults who thought that children were not ready for books until they could understand the stories being read to them.

But for a long time it seemed as if only librarians, teachers, children's book specialists, and professionals dealing with child development knew about the changes being made by publishers. Perhaps trusting too blindly in our education system, many parents left responsibility for cultivating interest in books and reading to the teachers.

Now it appears we have entered a wonderful new era when parents want to be part of their children's experience with books. They want to be involved in reading to their children, and they want to make the

1

best possible choices from the myriad books for pre-readers suddenly flooding the market.

But self-education in this area can be a nightmare. Imagine trying to sample, evaluate, or review every new book before buying or borrowing it to read to your child! The time and money required would make such screening impossible. Even scanning the many periodicals that review children's books—or asking every association which books *they* believe are the best for very young children—would be a time-consuming task. And one thing most new parents don't have is spare time. Even going to the local bookstore is not really a solution, because there are so many books to choose from. And rare is the bookstore clerk who *really knows* which books are best for children at the different stages of their development.

The aim of this book is to do all that legwork for you in two ways: by offering a basic list of books that are considered the best, and by giving you a set of guidelines to assist you in building your baby's library. In the process of writing it I discovered many groups and individuals all around the country—leaders of local parenting groups, book reviewers, librarians, and booksellers who specialize in the children's book area—who have been struggling to provide this sort of information for a smaller audience. I asked them to tell me which books they would want to tell all parents about—the books they believe are musts for every baby.

To be as useful as possible, this book combines the advice found in many of the parenting books that are familiar household "bibles" and the advice found in books about children's literature and reading. I have organized this handbook according to the generally accepted stages of a child's development. Few children reach a developmental stage on an exact timetable, but because the developmental *sequence* is similar for most children, this book can be followed in the order in which your child reaches each stage, regardless of his exact age.

The selection of recommended books is geared to appropriateness for the youngest age of each level. Thus, though an eight-year-old (or a forty-year-old, for that matter) can certainly gain meaning from *Where the Wild Things Are,* a four-year-old can enjoy this picture book by Maurice Sendak at a preliminary level.

I have chosen to end this sourcebook at the five-year-old category because by age five the average child will be attending some kind of school program on a regular basis, and the skills she acquires are greatly influenced by that single outside factor. This does not mean that parents shouldn't keep on using books at home with children over five years old! Other writers have treated the subject of the older child's need for books, and you should turn to these experts for guidance.

What this book is *not* about is how to teach your child to read at an early age. There are several books available on this subject; however, experts are divided over the wisdom and practicality of attempting to teach very young children how to read. What a first book experience should do for a child is strengthen the bonds between adult and child through sharing a story. It should stimulate a child's natural language development, which must be cultivated before reading can occur. And it should generally encourage children to feel comfortable with books, to accustom them to the look and feel of words on a page along with pictures that mean something. That is why it is important to have not only books that you read to your child, but also books that can be tossed around, tugged on, and washed or wiped clean.

But Is It a Book?

Books for infants and babies may seem at first to be an entirely different species from the traditional book an adult is accustomed to reading. In fact, a book for a one-year-old may sometimes look more like a bath toy than a book. But these forms serve a purpose. To be used and enjoyed by young children, the first books must be safe and reasonably indestructible.

Parents who want their child to derive full pleasure from a book not only will read to him from handsome "don't touch" volumes of classic rhymes but will also offer the child sturdy books that can stand up to teething, attempts to crumple, the pull-and-rip phase, and other wonderful forms of play in which books can be included.

For this reason many books are made of a durable cardboardlike material coated in nontoxic heavy gloss (referred to as board books). Some are even washable. Often produced in easy-to-hold (by a child) formats, they should have rounded corners that will not cut or poke the baby.

Cloth books are made of soft linen material. Some people favor these for young children, while others feel their lack of spine makes them frustrating. Perhaps for your child they will be a type of book to grow into. Babies like to test their newfound abilities. Don't let your six-month-old struggle too long with a cloth book, though; put it aside until he is ready to have fun with it. Its pliancy and comfort and virtual indestructibility may make it a better bet for him a month later.

You will also see many books that have a game-playing purpose. Some contain holes or slots for poking. There may be removable cardboard figures meant to be played with. (Don't give a baby any removable pieces if they might be swallowed.) Flaps can be lifted to reveal surprise pictures. Pop-up books contain three-dimensional illustrations that literally stand up from the pages of the book when the leaves are opened. In general, pop-ups should be reserved for after eighteen months, or they will be torn apart.

Still another form of book that calls for participation by the child invites him to touch the pages and feel different textures, or to remove stickers or colored plastic forms to be pasted down in other sections of the book—or wherever he feels the creative urge! You can bet the young child will exercise his imagination when it comes to making such decisions.

Why These Books?

I received much assistance in preparing the lists of recommended books. Every choice required a determination of the book's excellence or popularity—and preferably both. The suggestions for books to be included came from professionals who use children's books in working with parents and children, book reviewers, and members of organizations whose purpose is to promote reading, literature, or the education of young children.

Many of the selections appear here by unanimous choice. Others are the particular favorites of one person or another, and some are ground breakers—when published no books like them existed before.

Of all the books recommended to me, I have tried to choose a variety of fiction, informational books, concept books, classic stories, holiday tales, and poetry. There is no one kind of best book—there are good books of each kind, and there are individual children with different interests who may find one category more appealing than another. But most librarians will agree with me when I say that every child can benefit from exposure to the widest possible range of books.

Books are bridges to acquiring language, to coping with fears, to learning concepts, to exploring fantasies. No one would limit a child to any one of these experiences in her development—why limit your child to fairy tales? If your child sees only stories that depict animals as cute little walking, talking, elegantly dressed creatures, her view of animals may be lopsided. On the other hand, you needn't deluge her with discourses on natural science. There are simple board books that show beautifully rendered animals as they really are, living in their natural habitat, engaging in activities of their species. And picture books, even fiction, often show animals looking like the very real creatures we as adults know them to be. The bears we meet in Robert McCloskey's *Blueberries for Sal* are as realistic as any. And seeing bears acting as bears do gives a young child a healthy respect for natural law.

Where classic stories or fairy tales are concerned, there may be many different editions available. The artwork may vary widely, as will the size and shape of the books. Even the story may differ significantly in different editions. You should choose the one you find most appealing, and try different versions to see if the stories appeal more to your child in one form than in another. And if you have more than one child, it's an especially good idea to make sure each child's taste in books is cultivated. Just because one child liked one version of a classic doesn't necessarily mean it will have the same appeal for the second child.

Ultimately, of course, there is only *one best way* to buy books or select them from your library: Know your child and his abilities and interests, and choose accordingly. I hope this book will give you a head start in becoming familiar with the variety available. Soon regular trips to the bookstore or library will become an important family ritual that helps to deepen the reading habit. Once you see just how important books are to your child and to his development, and how reading with him can cement your relationship, you are likely to have many personal favorites to add to this list. Please pass them on to friends and relatives to give them their head start too!

A Word About Sexism in Children's Books

In the interest of making this book as nonsexist as possible, I have used the pronouns "he" and "she" interchangeably throughout. *Good Books to Grow On* is aimed at all parents and children, and I strongly feel that reading aloud to a child is an activity for fathers as well as mothers.

Fortunately, during the past ten years many children's books have been scrutinized for blatant sexism. Many of those that were found to include sexual stereotyping were rewritten or discontinued. Most of the books considered sexist were also so dated that they have fallen out of print. Yet some are still available in library collections, and if you are sensitive to this issue, I recommend that you do choose one of the many alternatives listed here. If, however, your child sees and likes a book that you find obnoxious, you may want to consider letting her read that along with one that treats the same theme in a nonsexist way. Try not to turn the child away from a book just because it seems to be offensive in this regard. As long as publishers continue to be aware of sexual stereotypes in books (if you find examples of it, write to the publisher and complain), the problem will diminish as time passes.

A Word About Licensed Characters

Books featuring cartoon-show characters or characters popularized as toys have become a major part of children's book publishing. Such familiar characters as "Care Bears," "Strawberry Shortcake," and "Muppet Babies" are referred to as licensed characters, and the storybooks written around them are usually part of the merchandising efforts of publishing companies, toy manufacturers, and television producers to saturate both the media and retail outlets with many different products related to the same characters.

The quality of books written as part of these merchandising programs varies, but because they are so heavily advertised on television, you will probably find that your child asks for or chooses these books before any others. Make sure you know what you are buying when you select these books—in some the art and stories may be quite captivating, while others are not as carefully made, and the underlying messages or themes may not be ones in which you believe.

Approach these books as you would sweets for your children: You must make your own decision about forbidding them, saving them as "treats," or letting your child dictate his consumption. Since I believe you should read to your child from a variety of books, if he likes the characters he sees in a cartoon show and wants to read a story about them, that's fine, as long as he is read to from many other kinds of books as well!

A Note Regarding Prices

All prices quoted for books listed in this collection were valid at the end of 1984. Alas, books, like everything else, are subject to inflation, and prices do go up. You may also find that prices vary from store to store, as many more booksellers have begun to discount their merchandise. The prices provided here offer only a sense of the approximate cost of the books, and you should not expect to find the books priced exactly as noted.

Chapter One

FROM BIRTH TO SIX MONTHS

*F*rom birth to six months old your baby goes through enormous changes in her mental, physical, and motor development. The newborn who could not reach for anything becomes the four-month-old with persistent, inconsistent, jerky motions, only to be transformed into the sure, quick-reaching six-month-old child.

By the time your baby is six months old, she will be able to inspect objects at length and can lift a cup by its handle. She also coos or hums and stops crying on hearing music—even reacts to changes in the volume of the stereo. The six-month-old is sophisticated enough to find interest in objects from different perspectives—right side up, upside down, or sideways.

By six months your baby distinguishes herself from you—and even from a mirror image of herself. She can also distinguish adults from children, and, in fact, may be disturbed by strangers of any age.

The major development of the four- to eight-month-old baby is the adaptation of specific practiced skills to the world around her. For example, opening and closing eyes is now valuable for use in social interaction, not just for seeing. Though your baby is learning about objects by testing them—poking, rolling, pushing—she has not yet developed the concept of the permanence of objects (or persons) in her world. She won't respond to your attempts to engage her in hide-and-seek games. She would much rather play pointing games. She likes to grab and pull as well—activities that foster her blossoming sensory development.

All of these movements, however, can only be accomplished if her head and hands are not required for any lower body maneuvering. Your baby has not yet learned to control her lower balance and uses her hands even to sit, so she cannot play or even suck her thumb from a standing position.

When you read to your newborn, it needn't always be while the baby is being readied for sleep. Some parents enjoy getting down on the rug with their baby, holding him on their tummies and having the other parent read some songs or poems or tell stories. This is a way of establishing the pattern for family story hours of future years. Many books today are also offered with accompanying cassette tapes. That may enable you to have a story playing as you show the book to your baby, letting you and the baby play with the book without sacrificing the words.

For now, books that appeal to your baby's bright-eyed curiosity with colorful pictures for him, but also with interest for you, are best bets. Now is the time to refresh your own memory of nursery rhymes, lullabies, classics, and perhaps favorites from your childhood. Many of the books suggested here are books I consider home library staples —Mother Goose treasuries, song collections, fairy tales. Some you will want to own for your home, and some you will prefer to borrow from the library. You might want to try several different versions of Mother Goose before purchasing the one you'd like to keep. Different illustrators can illuminate certain aspects of those rhymes in unique ways, but it also seems as if there is a Mother Goose for every taste, from formal to fanciful.

Look for books that you feel comfortable reading. Your baby will most likely be lying down as you read to him, so large books that you can read from and show to him are very good choices. Show him brightly colored pictures that attract his eye. Clean and simple ones are better than jumbled pictures because until three months babies do not see depth. Pages with one or two large illustrations are better than crowded pages with lots of activity.

The books best for babies to have nearby are cloth books, because you can leave them in the crib with him. For your baby's safety, don't let him near books with sharp edges or pages. Read those to him from a safe distance. Furthermore, make sure all cloth and tub books have the word *nontoxic* on them.

When you read to your child, try to memorize a line or two of a rhyme, a lullaby, a poem, or a particularly nice story. Speak these to your baby even when your book is not handy. Don't underestimate your baby by merely cooing to him. Give him all the richness of words. The sound he loves best right now is your voice, in all its tempos, cadences, and tones. Stories, songs, rhymes, and rhythmic prose give full vent to the range of your voice—use them for your baby's sake!

Baabee series by Dayal K. Khalsa. Tundra, 1983. $12.95 for a boxed set of four. **Here's Baabee, Baabee's Things, Baabee Gets Dressed,** and **Baabee's Home.** Based on the evidence that babies see two-dimensionally before they see depth, these are meant to be shown to babies to help them pick out shapes and colors at a very early age. They are accordion-folded and have holes that are designed for parents to thread string through so they can hang the books over a crib. The books are laminated, illustrated in seven pure colors, and show a symbolic baby of indeterminate sex or race in everyday surroundings, involved in everyday activities. Instructions are included for games adults and siblings can play with a baby.

Goodnight Moon by Margaret Wise Brown, pictures by Clement Hurd. Harper & Row, 1947. $7.89 hardcover, $2.95 paperback. This classic story of the little rabbit saying good night to all the familiar things in his room and outside his window has been pure enchantment for babies—and parents—as it weaves its spell over the ready-for-bed child. A lullaby in every sense of the word, this is a must for every home. If you start reading it early enough to your baby, you will find that some of her first words may be straight from this book. *The Goodnight Moon Room,* a pop-up version, is also available for older children.

Hosie's Aviary by Leonard Baskin. Viking Kestrel, 1979. $10.00. An art book and a book of poetry, this is also a book that pays tribute to exotic birds and animals. Its companion volume, *Hosie's Zoo*, treats more familiar beasts in the same manner, in watercolor with free-form prose poetry elaborating on the impressions conveyed by the paintings.

Hush Little Baby by Jeanette Winter. Pantheon, 1984. $10.95. Soft browns and muted reds and greens mingle with black-and-white illustrations to depict the story of the traditional bedtime lullaby. Text pages are bordered with details from each of the song's lines, and the book finishes off with the music for playing or singing the song.

Jump All the Morning: A Child's Day in Verse by P. K. Roche. Viking Kestrel, 1984. $9.95. You'll enjoy adding this to your collection of nursery rhymes to read aloud to your baby all the more because the rhymes show a young child's common activities, soon to be your baby's favorite topic.

The Little Drummer Boy, words and music by Katherine Davis, Henry Onorati, and Harry Simeone, illustrated by Ezra Jack Keats. Macmillan, 1968. $12.95 hardcover, $3.95 paperback. The popular Christmas song seems inspired by the illustrations of one of the best-loved children's illustrators. This song-storybook has right-hand piano accompaniment included for older piano-playing siblings to try out.

The Little Engine That Could by Watty Piper. Platt & Munk, 1930, 1961. $3.95. I list this as a first book for every home library because it has one of the most instantly recognizable lines in all of the children's books ever published. One new parent said that when he learned he was about to become a father, he went to a local bookseller and rather ashamedly said, "I'd like to buy some books to start my child off right. I don't remember any of the picture books I had as a kid, except for one. And would you believe I can't remember the name? But it had a line that went like this: 'I think I can, I think I can, I think I can.' " The bookseller smiled and instantly pulled out a copy of *The Little Engine That Could*. "That's it!" the father cried. But he still looked puzzled, turning page after page, until finally he came to the ending and actually read those words again for himself. "That's it," he said, now satisfied. "This is the book I want to read to my kid."

The Little Engine That Could: Deluxe Peggy Cloth Book. Platt & Munk, 1980. $3.95. The story of the Little Blue Engine who uses the power of positive thinking to pull a load up a mountain is here printed on cloth. The colors, all bright and flat, should attract the eyes of even newborns, and the soft cloth makes it a crib toy as well as a book. The publisher also released a pop-up version of this classic for $6.95.

Little Treasury of Peter Rabbit, retold by Corey Nash, with Beatrix Potter illustrations. Crown, 1983. $4.98. Six sturdy little board books offer babies the opportunity to get hands-on experience with those wonderful Potter characters, Peter Rabbit and Benjamin Bunny.

Lullabies and Night Songs. Harper & Row, 1965. $22.00. A book for parents to use as a resource, or to treasure and keep, this eighty-page volume is illustrated in full color by the Caldecott artist Maurice Sendak. Will Engvich, the editor, has selected nursery rhymes, ballads, poems, and lullabies from around the world for inclusion, and Alec Wilder has provided music for piano accompaniment.

Lullaby of the Wind by Karen Whiteside, pictures by Kazue Mizumura. Harper & Row, 1984. $9.95. A soft and graceful book, this is like the wind it tells of. The wind blows out the flame of the candle, gently pushes over land and sea, and sings a child to sleep.

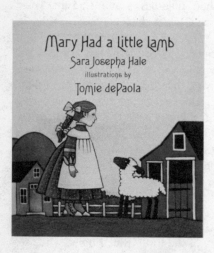

Marguerite de Angeli's Book of Nursery and Mother Goose Rhymes. Doubleday, 1953. $12.95 hardcover, $5.95 paperback. English countryside-inspired illustrations have an olden-days look, with many of the children depicted as rosy-cheeked cherubs softly sketched among the rhymes. Here is a generous collection both in size and content (376 rhymes), with bursts of warmly colored plates mingled with black-and-white drawings.

Mary Had a Little Lamb by Sara Josepha Hale, illustrated by Tomie dePaola. Holiday House, 1984. $13.95 hardcover, $5.95 paperback. The words to the song and its music start the book off. DePaola's colors are beautiful, suggesting the old-fashioned look of woodcuts, and balance appropriately with the historical perspective he adds to the book by including a bit of lore about how the song came to be.

Mother Goose by Gyo Fujikawa. Grosset and Dunlap, 1968, 1982. $5.95. Seventy-seven pages of long and short rhymes in a large lap-size book are sweetly and softly illustrated by the popular artist.

"The Old Woman in a Shoe" is particularly well done, giving an open-ended view of the shoe house with babies beginning to be tucked cozily into bed.

Other Mother Goose Treasuries of Note

Mother Goose by Tasha Tudor. Walck, 1944. $8.95. Here is a Mother Goose version that will bring all the charms of English Romanticism to your family. Tudor's old-fashioned, sweet illustrations bring out yet another side of the seventy-seven verses she has collected in this book.

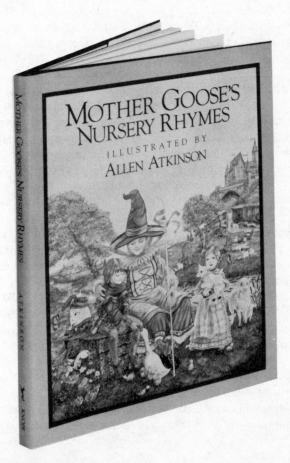

Mother Goose's Nursery Rhymes by Allen Atkinson. Knopf, 1984. $13.95. The lush colors of Atkinson's art for this book make all the nursery rhymes come alive with a wash of dawn-colored gold and rose tones. Even the insides of the book's covers have been beautifully painted for the reader's pleasure.

Mother Goose Treasury by Raymond Briggs. Coward, McCann, 1966. $16.95. Higher priced than some others, this is nevertheless a beautiful household keepsake, with 408 rhymes and 897 illustrations.

The Real Mother Goose, illustrated by Blanche Fisher Wright. Rand McNally, 1944. $8.95. From "Little Bo Peep" to "Sulky Sue" to "Three Blind Mice," this volume contains almost 300 rhymes —literally a one-volume Mother Goose library. Illustrations are in the classic tradition—all in color, some full-page pictures, some spot illustrations. All are beauties.

The Night Before Christmas by Clement Moore, illustrated by Tomie dePaola. Holiday House, 1980. $12.95 hardcover, $4.95 paperback. Because the well-known poem is practically part of our American heritage, it seems that this book turns up on nearly every list of basic home library books. What dePaola brings to it is also truly American. He has set the story in the 1840s and given it that very old-fashioned flavor of early American art. Very bright, each page is bordered with different patterns found in New England quilts.

The Original Peter Rabbit Books® by Beatrix Potter. Frederick Warne, 1902–1922. $3.95 each. The tales of Peter Rabbit, Benjamin Bunny, Jemima Puddle-Duck, and the Flopsy Bunnies date back to the turn of the century and have endured with strength for their warmth and imagination. There are twenty-three tales in all, and the set is a collection of small hardcover books that make a wonderful home library for children to grow on. The publisher has also made the first twelve in the series available in paperback for $2.25 each.

The Tale of Peter Rabbit and Other Stories by Beatrix Potter, illustrated by Allen Atkinson. Knopf, 1984. $16.95. Another gorgeous edition of Beatrix Potter's wonderful rabbit tales, Atkinson's is larger and more lush than the originals. As with other famous collections that exist in many different styles, you should choose the one you find most appealing, and try different versions to see if the tales have different appeal for your child if the illustrations vary. In the case of the tales of Peter Rabbit, Atkinson's edition would certainly coexist well with Beatrix Potter's, being unique enough to give the works a different flavor.

Pillow Pals by Lin Howard. Platt & Munk, 1984. $4.95 each. Two titles, *Hello Baby* and *Baby Talk,* present a new concept in soft toys that are also books. These machine-washable percale foam-stuffed "pillows" actually unfold to become storybooks, with art printed in vivid nontoxic inks on the fabric.

Poems to Read to the Very Young, selected by Josette Frank, illustrated by Eloise Wilkin. Random House, 1982. $5.95. Seventy jewels from traditional and modern selections, made for sharing and brought to sweet life by Wilkin's work.

Pooh's Bedtime Book by A. A. Milne, illustrated by Ernest H. Shepard. Dutton, 1980. $7.95. Here is a compilation of some favorites ("Us Too," "Sneezles," "Winnie-the-Pooh," and "Some Bees") from Milne that you will enjoy reading to your infant, especially if you like Milne but don't want to read aloud from the longer books. The selections are collected in a large lap-size book filled with Ernest H. Shepard's magical illustrations, beautifully hand-colored.

Prayer for a Child by Rachel Field, illustrated by Elizabeth Orton Jones. Macmillan, 1945. $8.95 hardcover, $3.95 paperback. A Caldecott Medal Winner (1945). The simple beauty of a child's prayer captures the faith and trust of children everywhere.

Pudgy Series of Board Books by various authors. Grosset and Dunlap, 1983, 1984. $2.95 each. Among these full-color, die-cut board books are *The Pudgy Book of Babies,* illustrated by Kathy Wilburn, *The Pudgy Book of Farm Animals,* illustrated by Julie Durrell, and *The Pudgy Bunny Book,* illustrated by Ruth Sanderson. Likely the most engaging for using with your newborn is *The Pudgy Rock-a-Bye Book,* illustrated by Kathy Wilburn. In a small, sturdy, hand-size board book, familiar bedtime story rhymes like "Star Light, Star

THE
RANDOM HOUSE
Book of
POETRY
for Children

A Treasury of 572 Poems
for Today's Child

SELECTED BY
JACK PRELUTSKY

ILLUSTRATED BY
ARNOLD LOBEL

Bright'' are illustrated sweetly. The rhymes are punctuated by drawings of freshly scrubbed, ready-for-bed, sleepy babies and kittens, the peaceful night sky, and other drowsy scenes.

The Random House Book of Poetry for Children, selected by Jack Prelutsky, illustrated by Arnold Lobel. Random House, 1983. $13.95. A treasure chest of 572 poems from past and present, arranged in fourteen thematic sections. Pick out one or two just for starters, and progress with others as the children in your life grow—this book will grow with them. Not only does it look inviting, which should encourage adults to delve into it for read-aloud verse, but it's lots of fun. Prelutsky's natural ear for humor shows through. You'll laugh out loud, and such joy can only contribute to your children's natural inclination for the rhymes and rhythms of poetry. And to top it all off, the variety of subjects covered—people, city, home, animals, seasons, nature, nonsense—ensures that it provides something for everyone of all ages.

Singing Bee!, compiled by Jane Hart, illustrated by Anita Lobel. Lothrop, Lee & Shepard, 1982. $16.00. A treasury of 125 songs, new and old, for all the occasions of your child's life—enjoy them for yourself too. Includes simple piano arrangements and guitar chords.

The Story of Babar by Jean de Brunhoff. Random House, 1960. $12.95. A must for every starter home library, Babar's story is one of wonderfully droll amusement, and it begins a lifetime relationship with the elephant and his progeny. In this introductory tale Babar's mother is killed by a hunter, so he runs away to a town, where he suits himself up and goes to live with a rich old woman. After having some city experiences, he goes home to marry Celeste and become King of the Elephants.

The Sun's Asleep Behind the Hill by Mirra Ginsburg, illustrated by Paul O. Zelinsky. Greenwillow, 1982. $10.25. A lullaby story you'll be able to enjoy reading and looking at yourself for its lushly sleep-inducing, dusky-colored paintings. But the illustrations provide only half the charm of this book, for the cumulative story of the breeze stilling, the bird quieting, the squirrel sleeping, the child resting, until finally the moon shines alone in the night sky, is a peaceful and comforting tale to hear.

Tasha Tudor's Bedtime Book. Platt & Munk, 1977. $6.95. Prose and poetry are both included here, and most are old, recognizable favorites—"Goldilocks," "Snow White," "The Shoemaker and the Elves," to mention a few. Tasha Tudor's style of illustration is also likely to be recognized, with her soft pastels and English country garden settings, just right for quieting down restless children at bedtime.

Chapter Two
FROM SIX MONTHS TO ONE YEAR

*J*t is in the second half of the baby's first year that he will be ready to use his body in a more controlled way. In fact, at an earlier age it may have seemed as if he were fighting with himself to accomplish certain tasks. These will now be done with ease.

For example, while a six-month-old reaches with a whole-hand scooping motion, the eight-month-old can use his fingers and thumbs to grasp objects and to hold on to them. By nine months he is likely to have the fine control over separate fingers that allows him to use them to point or poke. At the same time he learns to grasp, he is developing the ability to release what he grasps—so that in his tenth or eleventh month the baby may seem to be constantly dropping things. He is exercising his newfound freedom to uncurl his fingers!

By this point a baby will demonstrate an interest in touching and stroking and will enjoy feeling the differences in textures.

Two other simultaneous developments in the second half of the first year coordinate with new kinds of play you will find your child enjoying: The baby can reach accurately for objects while looking away from them, and can remember events and things for longer and longer periods of time. Peekaboo and hide-and-seek now become games for your baby to participate in, not just observe.

Language development is now crucial—and astounding. It is at this period of your baby's life that he is learning language, though he cannot yet speak. First, before he can speak, he must listen to what you say and learn the meaning of the words you use. While your baby is learning to listen to language, and as he begins to develop the sounds we call babbling—which later will become vowels, consonants, and words—he is learning as well to recognize emotions in the voice of the speaker and to express emotions himself. He is developing the ability to express the full range of his personality, from a sense of humor to a sense of negativism.

Reaching all of these new stages can be reflected in your reading with your child. And, in turn, reading with your child encourages these developmental milestones. As she becomes more agile with her hands, the physical act of turning the pages of a book becomes a game to master. Now, too, she can look at the pictures on those pages with interest. At the same time she is learning from your voice, and what you read to her, all the emotions that can be expressed in a story. For adults who may feel constrained to chatter away to a baby who cannot respond in sentences, reading is the kind of activity that can promote talk between parent and child while allowing them to retain a sense of dignity.

Make sure your choice of books for the baby herself to hold is geared to the books' sturdiness, because some are apt to be easily torn, tugged, soaked, or shredded apart. It's a wise idea to keep a baby away from family library sets of nice hardcover books and to read to her from those only when she won't want to touch them. But because many of the classics are available in inexpensive or paperback editions, you may want to get one for "real" use and one for safe-keeping. As your child grows older, she can enjoy the nicer books. And having a grown-up-looking set of classics around is one way to ensure that your child keeps on reading wonderfully rich childhood favorites. Older children frequently reject books as looking too "baby-ish." But big hardcovers printed on nice paper certainly won't turn a child off for that reason.

Nevertheless, these are not the best books to put in reach of a very young child. Books that give you the opportunity to form interesting sounds—animal noises, noises of household objects—are fun for your baby. Books that encourage games like peekaboo are appropriate choices now. Ones that can withstand baby handling are the wisest buys. What is key at this point is getting your child accustomed to books. Books should be as much a part of a child's early experience as dolls, blocks, and rattles. At six months a child is fascinated by the simple sight of a page that turns and has pictures on it—so books with heavy cardboard pages that open easily for her prove amazing fun. Watch her shut the book or let it fall with delight!

Still, the books that you read to her, and those that let her hear you singing or saying rhymes, are books of deep and satisfying pleasure for your baby. Share the experience of language with her, and use books as the means for that experience.

Alphabears by Kathleen Hague, illustrated by Michael Hague. Holt, Rinehart & Winston, 1984. $10.45. For each letter of the alphabet there is a bear, whose unique qualities are described in lilting rhyming couplets and pictured in glorious detail that will be fun to look at many times over.

Animal Noises by Sally Kilroy. Four Winds Press, 1983. $4.95. This board book names the sounds made by familiar, joyfully drawn animals such as the cow pictured on the book's cover. A baby will love hearing the sounds *moo, meow, squeak, buzz,* and so on again and again, learning to imitate them. Sally Kilroy is also the author of several other first board books: *Baby Colors, Babies' Bodies,* and *Noisy Homes. Noisy Homes* names many of the sounds your baby is likely to hear (or create) at home. A picture of a baby laughing is

labeled "tee-hee," while another baby, crying, says "boo-hoo." It all ends with the happy sounds of a baby in his tub: *splish, splash,* a rubber duck and a sailboat dancing on the water. Of this group, *Baby Colors* is slightly more advanced than its companions, because the concept of colors having names is definitely a step up, and this book shows patterns as well as simple colors. Of course, the words themselves are fun to hear and are likely to tickle your baby's fancy.

Anno's Alphabet by Mitsumasa Anno. T. Y. Crowell, 1975. $10.89. Subtitled "An Adventure in Imagination," this truly amazing alphabet book uses capital letters that give the illusion of having been carved from solid oak. The artist has captured so startlingly well the look and, so it seems, *feel* of wood! Borders detail many objects beginning with the same letter. Also by the author: *Anno's Counting Book,* 1977, $10.89.

Baabee books, second series. **Baabee Goes Out, Baabee Plays, Baabee Takes a Bath, Goodnight, Baabee** by Dayal K. Khalsa. Tundra, 1983. $12.95 for a boxed set of four. A second level of the infants' books, these open like regular books, not accordion-folded as the first set is (see page 11), and continue to show the two-dimensional symbolic baby in everyday happenings.

Baby Ben Books by Harriet Ziefert, illustrated by Norman Gorbaty. Random House, 1984. $2.95 each. **Bow-Wow, Busy, Go-Go,** and **Noisy**. A two-dimensional baby pictured in bold colors in these laminated board books, Baby Ben is a definite personality, not a symbolic character. He can dig, make animal noises, make his toys go *beep, toot,* and *zoom,* and he plays games babies love.

Baby's First Books: On the Farm and **Big and Little.** Grosset and Dunlap, 1978. $2.25 each. Line drawings in these books illustrate concepts, which will make them useful later on in your baby's life, and show animals and people in a distinguishable style. They make good early "references" (particularly the animals in *On the Farm,* because the pictures are accurate without being too complex).

Block Books: Set I by Lawrence Di Fiori, **Set II** by Robert Highsmith. Macmillan, 1983. $2.95 each. Eight sturdy board books designed to appeal to children just beginning to connect words and objects, these will provide a good basis for vocabulary building at later stages. With simple, bright pictures, words name everyday objects and places that a baby will soon be familiar with. *Set I* includes *Baby Animals, The Farm, My First Book,* and *My Toys. Set II* includes *My Town, Wheels, By the Seashore,* and *The Zoo.*

Dressing by Helen Oxenbury. Simon & Schuster, 1981. $3.50. Another gem of a board book done in soft colors, with one word and picture per page. First we see a diaper, then we see the baby dressed in the diaper. And so it goes, from undershirt up to overalls, and at the end the baby is all dressed to go outside. A wonderful first book for introducing your child to the names of clothing—and your child will love looking at the baby Oxenbury so charmingly illustrates.

Early Morning in the Barn by Nancy Tafuri. Greenwillow, 1983. $10.50. A glorious tribute to the early morning sights and sounds found in a barn, this is a large book with its pages filled to the edges with animals drawn on a grand scale. What makes it nice for such young babies is that all the animals are black-outlined, for easy distinction, yet the colors are not scrimped on in favor of the simplicity of the style. Shapes are easily distinguishable, and though sounds are the only words written on the pages, the book vibrates with life.

Family by Helen Oxenbury. Simon & Schuster, 1981. $3.50. Father, with baby snuggling inside his overcoat, is the first person cozily pictured in this small board book, which depicts some of the people in direct relationship to a very young baby.

Golden Block Books. Western Publishing, 1982. $3.50 each. Looking just like children's blocks, they are stackable when closed because they are made of heavy board pages.

The books are stiff enough to stand open to look at. Bright full-color illustrations introduce favorite subjects. *The ABC Book* by Robbie Stillerman shows alphabet letters and whimsical pictures of animals and objects. *Count to Ten* by Marc Brown will be useful for counting later on, but also introduces objects babies will be becoming familiar with now. The same is true of the objects in *First Things*—a cup, a spoon, a telephone, a tricycle—illustrated by Virginia Parsons. *Animal Babies* by Simon Galkin introduces kittens, puppies, lambs, and so on. A useful play toy and book combination.

Kittens Are Like That by Jan Pfloog. Random House, 1976. $1.50 paperback. Who can resist lovable, playful kittens, sweet as any baby, in their daily play?

The Moon by Robert Louis Stevenson, pictures by Denise Saldutti. Harper & Row, 1984. $10.95. A haunting, glowingly illustrated tale of what happens by the light of the moon. Stevenson's elegant yet ear-catching poem will be one more that verse-loving children will find easy to bed down to.

Muppet Babies Take a Bath by Manhar Chauhan. Random House, 1984. $2.95. The popular Jim Hensen characters appear as they might have looked in babyhood—with all their endearing personality traits, cutely drawn.

Numbers of Things by Helen Oxenbury. Delacorte, 1983. $12.95. From one lion, two old-fashioned cars, and three children, on through ten, twenty, thirty, and fifty sets of like objects, Helen Oxenbury shows cleverly not only the similarities but the differences in objects with the same name. The pictures seem never to be static, but always to hold something to be discovered. Note, though, that the British *ladybird* has not been changed to the more familiar *ladybug,* of which we find fifty adorable ones (a favorite childhood bug) at the end of the book.

Peek-a-Boo! by Janet and Allan Ahlberg. Viking Kestrel, 1981. $10.95 hardcover, $3.50 paperback. A full page and a page with a hole in it alternate to give a small child a peekaboo look at the details of different warm family scenes. Rhyming verse to read to your baby asks questions and gives answers about what is pictured in the scene. Because it keeps to a baby's point of view, it's a marvelous eye-opener for adults, as well as being perfectly well geared to the child in your life.

Peek-a-Boo: I See You! by Joan Phillips, illustrated by Kathy Wilburn. Grosset and Dunlap, 1983. $3.95. A tall board book, this is a wonderful, easy-to-repeat rhyme that incorporates a game of peek-aboo. Toddlers can point out who's hiding and laugh with the exuberant children pictured, joining in their fun.

Peter Spier's Little Animal Books. Doubleday/Balloon Books, 1984. $10.00 for boxed set of four, also sold individually for $2.50 each. Spier's art brings life to all these little animals, your baby's favorites— *Little Rabbits, Little Cats, Little Ducks,* and *Little Dogs.* While there are so many board books in this category, Spier's illustrations are so unfailingly cheerful and easy to look at that these make a perfect gift, even for a baby who is flooded with others—because these books seem to become old friends, enjoyed long after others are grown tired of.

Play Kitten by Emanuel Schongut. Simon & Schuster, 1983. $3.95. A simply drawn but lively kitten is seen from a toddler's perspective playing with and upsetting various toys. This floor-height view of a kitten's antics makes an interesting experiment of picturing the way a crawling baby would actually view the scene—a refreshing pose.

Sing and Read Musical Books: Mary Had a Little Lamb, The Farmer in the Dell, Yankee Doodle, and **Teensy Weensy Spider.** Modern Promotions, 1984. $4.98 each.

These board books come equipped with a cell that allows the melody of each of these songs to play when the book is opened—and to stop when it is closed. Great attention-grabbers, they are liked by mothers who have bought them for the pretty art, the novelty, the books' sturdiness, and also because they serve to establish a connection between fun and books in the baby's mind.

When the Dark Comes Dancing: A Bedtime Poetry Book, compiled by Nancy Larrick, illustrated by John Wallner. Philomel, 1983. $15.95. This collection can be read to babies even as young as six months, but it surely goes way above that in its appeal. Some of the poems are soothing, some are lilting, some can be enjoyed just for the pure sound of the words (and the baby will love hearing your voice moving in rhythm)—others are to be savored for their meaning as well. The works of Robert Louis Stevenson, Christina Rossetti, Vachel Lindsay, and many others are included in this collection that tells of the moon and stars, little creatures falling fast asleep, odes to the end of day, and even a lullaby of raindrops. The exquisitely jeweled colors and black-and-white illustrations add to the dreamlike charm of this collection.

Working by Helen Oxenbury. Simon & Schuster, 1981. $3.50. Potty, carriage, bowl, bathtub, crib—some of these may not be in your baby's world, but the pictures in this board book are clearly important in the daily routine of the baby who's the focus of these pages.

Chapter Three

FROM ONE YEAR TO EIGHTEEN MONTHS

*B*y now the infant who came into your lives one year ago has dramatically changed into the toddler, with an entirely new perspective on her world. Now that she can walk, she will begin to experiment with all she finds as she moves about. Everything must be discovered, including many things that might have once seemed familiar. They may appear entirely different to your toddler as she looks on them from different distances, different angles, or as she begins to understand some of their many properties. She is beginning to *conceptualize* about her world.

In the process the toddler is not only discovering what is around her—its hardness or softness, whether or not it bounces or makes noise, and so forth—but she is also learning new skills to use in dealing with those characteristics of objects. And she will be practicing all the skills she masters.

The thirteen-month-old who is still in the phase of taking things apart (and off, such as her clothes) will shortly begin to learn to put things together. She can build a tower of two cubes. She will try to fill empty boxes with objects, or to wedge one object into another. This play is also learning. At this age all the toddler sees, hears, and does is part of her learning experience, and part of her play as well.

According to Frank and Theresa Caplan, in their book *The Second Twelve Months of Life,* parents need to be aware of the critical periods of growth and development in their toddler, when newly emerging skills are in need of challenge and ample opportunities to use them. It is clearly better to overchallenge a toddler, but not to the point of frustration.

The toddler's memory is now developing, though it is still short, and she will progress from her joy and ability with peekaboo games to hiding and chase games as she begins to remember and find hidden objects and people and to delight in retrieving things over and over.

Because language acquisition depends not only on listening but also on all the child's senses and experiences with people, all that your toddler learns at this point has bearing on learning language. He learns that what and who he sees and touches can be named. Then he learns to put words to concepts such as "up," "down," "soft," and "hard." Finally he can make a correlation between images of objects and their physical presence and know that they are the same. He can identify pictures of dogs and understand that they are the same as the dog next door and is called by the same word. When he looks at the picture, says "dog," and imitates the dog's barking sound, he has made a huge leap in linking language and meaning.

By the age of eighteen months your child will suddenly seem to explode into a talking child, something he has been preparing for, and for which you have been readying him by introducing him to as many experiences as possible.

In choosing books for your toddler, bear in mind how his thinking is developing. Observe what he has previously enjoyed, and use that as a guideline. Know, too, that at this point change is a positive factor in his learning. Just as you would give him different toys to play with, choose different books to read to your child, to look at with him, or to give the toddler to look at for himself—an idea for times when he isn't mobile, such as when he's in his crib. He has enjoyed rhymes and jingles since the start of this period. By the age of fifteen months he has a sense of humor and is at the threshold of developing an imagination. Use stories, music, and toys to help him stretch that imagination.

You may feel frustrated if the baby who sat still for an entire story as you read it does not want to be so passive in his toddler months. He will want to pick out and point to pictures, listen to you talk about them, pat the objects, feel textured pictures, and help you turn the pages. Picture books with big and detailed illustrations may help hold the toddler's attention more readily, because there is more to see and name on a page. This variety of images is important. Photo picture books can show the toddler images close to the reality of his world, while storybooks introducing letters and numbers are also appropriate now, because counting games will begin to have some meaning.

Baby Socks by Anne Baird. William Morrow, 1984. $3.95. A board book in the *Wee William* series, its die-cut shape and bright colors should capture toddlers' attention. Like one of its series companions, *Kiss, Kiss,* this focuses on one of the endearing traits of babies: Here, socks are for anything but feet. *Kiss, Kiss* focuses on the baby's natural inclination toward being affectionate, and will remind many parents of their children.

But Not the Hippopotamus by Sandra Boynton. Simon & Schuster, 1982. $3.50. A small board book by the popular humorist, this sweet and funny rhyming story concerns a lone hippopotamus who watches all the other animals having fun, until at last he is invited to join them. A good recommendation for a short but very satisfying read-aloud for one- to two-year-olds. Others in this series are *The Going to Bed Book; Moo, Baa, La La La;* and *Opposites*.

A Child's First Book of Poems, pictures by Cyndy Szekeres. Western Publishing, 1981. $6.95. Beautiful endpapers picture a field of flowers and tiny animals. Inside, all the poems also have something to do with animals, which the art picks up and even embellishes. Some poems are humorous, some are straightforward, and others are pure flights of imagination. Pick out one for a short sitting, or just go through the mice and puppies and pigs that gaily decorate the pages and illustrate the poems. Kids of the youngest age won't need any encouragement to become involved in this pretty book.

Dear Zoo by Rod Campbell. Four Winds Press, 1983. $5.95. A lift-the-flap book that has proved pure delight for one-year-olds. It all begins with "I wrote to the zoo to send me a pet." The toddler can easily pull down the flaps himself to reveal all the funny animals that arrive in crates and boxes: a giraffe (too tall!), a monkey (too naughty!),

a frog (too jumpy!). At last the perfect pet arrives in a carrying case: a little puppy, just right for any child. At the request of a fifteen-month-old, I recently gave a copy to her cousin of sixteen months, so "Vanessa have *Dear Zoo*" too!

Ernie's Bath Book. Random House, 1983. $2.50. A soft, non-toxic vinyl book made for bathtime play, this has Sesame Street's Ernie describing tub fun in jaunty verses, with Rubber Duckie over-seeing the bathtime routine.

The First Words Picture Book by Bill Gilham, illustrated with photographs by Sam Grainger. Coward, McCann, 1982. $7.95 hardcover, $3.95 paperback. A picture of an object is captioned with its name. To the right is a photograph of the object in some context, with a simple one-line explanation. The clear photographs should intrigue one-year-olds as much as the words themselves, particularly because the scenes are pertinent to young children's everyday worlds. You'll also notice that as your child grows more interested in other children, she will return to these photos to make comments about the pictures of the kids shown here!

Goodnight, Goodnight by Eve Rice. Greenwillow, 1980. $9.95 hardcover, $3.50 Puffin Books paperback. All over town people

are saying good night as darkness falls, while one little lone cat on the roof longs for someone to come and play. At last his mother finds him, and then the two of them say good night to each other. What a wonderful book for assuring babies of their mothers' love at the end of the day.

Henry's Busy Day by Rod Campbell. Viking Kestrel, 1984. $6.95. Action words and lively pictures show a baby how Henry the cat spends his day. Encourages child involvement: Kids can pat Henry's soft, furry coat as he sleeps in his basket at the end of the book. A good accompaniment to the texture-boxes (homemade kits filled with materials of various texture) your child will be enjoying, and to the classic *Pat the Bunny* (see page 36).

I Am a Little Lion, I Am a Little Elephant, and **I Am a Little Dog** by Amrei Fechner; **I Am a Little Cat** by Helmut Spanner. Barron's, 1984. $4.95. Each of these titles depicts a day in the young animal's life, as told by the animal. A large-size format printed on heavy cardboard stock makes these books long-wearing.

Lowly Worm Word Book by Richard Scarry. Random House, 1981. $2.95. A Chunky Book. Lowly Worm appears on each page in the capacity of tour guide as he introduces the toddler to all kinds of "point and say" everyday words. The variety of words and the number per page make this a good follow-up for toddlers who have outgrown one-word-per-page board books.

Natural Pop-ups by Graham Tarrant, illustrated by Tony King. Putnam's, 1983, 1984. $6.95 each. **Butterflies, Frogs, Honeybees,** and **Rabbits**. The colorfully striking, (and, importantly) scientifically accurate pictures that fill these various pop-ups are what make them so recommended for youngsters of this age. The pop-up element only enhances their beauty, and while the text may be a bit much for one-year-olds, read it to them anyway—you'll find you will learn some interesting information yourself, and later you will be surprised to see how much your child has absorbed if he becomes fascinated by the books, as he most surely will.

1, 2, 3 to the Zoo by Eric Carle. Philomel, 1968. $5.95 paperback. Colorful double-page art contains a numeral and a corresponding number of animals. Eric Carle's bold art is irresistible, with all the animals pictured zoo-bound in a train car that grows as more and more creatures are brought on board.

Pat the Bunny by Dorothy Kunhardt. Western Publishing, 1940. $4.95. A Golden Book. This is the classic spiral-bound cardboard book that preceded all others in encouraging all of a developing child's interest in the realm of the senses. Your child will touch the different textures inside the outlines and also smell the flower, which has been scented. Looking in the mirror, lifting the cloth flap to play peekaboo— these are activities that will keep your child fascinated for hours, and this kind of active book experience also makes her feel that a book is fun, leading not only to an interest in other books of the touch-and-feel variety, but also to a positive feeling toward books in general. A new release is *Pat the Cat* by Edith Kunhardt.

Peek-a-Boo ABC by Demi. Random House, 1982. $4.95. For nimble-fingered preschoolers, or for younger children with an adult to help, this ABC book offers the delights of lift-the-flap and peekaboo games. The device used is an ark, which is also the *A* word. Open its doors and animals from *B* to *Z* appear—that will keep a youngster involved in alphabet-learning fun.

The Pudgy Finger Counting Book, illustrated by Doug Cashman. Grosset and Dunlap, 1983. $2.95. This board book gives babies the opportunity to play a Ten Little Indians–style game and learn some counting skills too. "Pudgies" are what is counted—little fingertip puppet animals—that adults may want to recreate at home for an extension of the fun found in the book. Enjoy!

Spot's Toys: A Soft Spot Book by Eric Hill. Putnam's, 1984. $2.95. A bathtime book, by the original creator of Spot the dog, allows Spot to join in bathtime routines and tells all about Spot's favorite playthings and the games he enjoys.

Titus Bear Goes to Bed by Renate Kozikowski. Harper & Row, 1984. $2.95. When kids have outgrown the one-picture, one-word-per-page board book, Titus will show them something more. As the main character in this simple-sentence, simple-action board book, he demonstrates all the independence desired by babies struggling to accomplish growth tasks.

The Touch Me Book by Pat and Eve Witte, illustrated by Harlow Rockwell. Western Publishing, 1961. $4.95. A spiral-bound book with questions to be answered by feeling the textures on the pages. What feels soft? Fur is soft, a puppy is soft, a kitten is soft. Explores hard, bumpy, spongy, and encourages a child's continuing explorations of those and other textures when you're done reading the book. Similarly *Soft As a Kitten* by Audean Johnson, a board book that is a catalyst for a child's learning about the world of the senses, shows how to name and describe those senses.

What's Teddy Bear Doing? illustrated by Helmut Spanner. Price/Stern/Sloan, 1983. $1.50. Wordless pictures of a friendly fuzzy bear show him riding his tricycle, watering his plant, sweeping up. You can make a game of this by inventing stories to go with each picture, and later you can ask your child what Teddy's doing and soon hear him give you his own version of what's going on.

Where's Spot? by Eric Hill. Putnam's, 1980. $9.95. Sally, a mother dog, searches for Spot all around the house and uncovers quite a few surprises in this lift-the-flap board book that continues your

child's enjoyment of peekaboo and hiding games. Alligator under the bed, penguins in the toy chest, and more introduce your toddler to new animals as well, before Spot is gleefully discovered eating from his bowl. Perfect humor for toddlers. Also, *Spot's First Walk, Spot's Birthday Party,* and *Spot's First Christmas,* $9.95 each. All are available in Spanish editions as well.

Who Said Meow? by Maria Polushkin, pictures by Giulio Maestro. Crown, 1975. $5.95. A very large book (more than eight inches by eleven inches) filled out with large characters. Puppy hears a *meow* one morning and asks all the neighborhood animals who said it. Meanwhile we see a frisky little cat just out of sight, and we can't wait until Puppy figures out that's who's making that noise. The sweet ending caps it off.

Chapter Four

FROM EIGHTEEN MONTHS TO TWO YEARS

*T*he period from eighteen months to two years in your toddler's development is most likely characterized as one of expansion of his repertoire of abilities. He is now at a point where he is refining his abilities and is able to perform more than one function at a time or pay attention to other things while he is moving around. By eighteen months old, he will be able to move from a sitting to a standing position without help. While he walks he can carry a toy, and can bend down and pick up something else and carry it, too, perhaps laying down the first one at some other point. And if at the same time he hears you call, he can turn his head to listen.

After months of wandering through his world, the toddler's exploring has changed to experimenting, and this extends from the external experiments with the physical world to internal experimenting as well. That is, he is developing a memory and testing it. He has seen that the ball rolls away when the door opens, and that the tower of blocks topples when the bottom block is removed, and he knows those things without having to test them out over and over. Amazingly, he begins to translate his knowledge into a mental representation of the outcome. All his experimenting in the present is becoming part of his memory of past experience, which he uses on his way to achieving a sense of object permanence. His increasing skills in imitation are another manifestation of his developing senses. He first imitates activities as he sees others performing them, but later on begins imitating them at other times. You may see him imitate the chatter of adults when the two of you are alone. He may imitate eating rituals he has seen at the table, or cleaning, or other ordinary daily routines. By the age of two many children are beginning to enjoy make-believe play, and books can help them develop this impulse.

Simultaneously the toddler's acquisition of language is growing, so that between eighteen months and two years he begins to use two-word phrases. Noun and verb phrases soon follow, and personal pronouns come as well. He may begin to understand when you name feelings for him, even if he cannot yet follow suit. The toddler by now is familiar with everyday sounds and is fascinated by them. You can help him name what he hears not only inside the house, but outside as well, and finally the noises of animals or things he sees pictures of but which will not be in his everyday realm of experience. At this age toddlers are particularly interested in their own environment, though, and especially in the smallest things in it. While some may love animals and birds, others have reached the stage of developing phobias, of which dogs head the list.

The toddler continues to enjoy nursery rhymes and songs. Now that her fine motor development is better, finger games and finger rhymes become popular, as do picture-card matching games. Have a story or rhyme to go along with these pastimes, because the toddler of twenty-two months has begun to be able to grasp the rudiments of a story line. When you read to her, read slowly, so that she can have time to understand what's happening in the story.

However, she will still love pointing to the familiar pictures, naming what she knows, and answering questions you ask her about what she sees on the page. Give her the time to participate in the book in this way, as long as her attention span holds. Her fascination with visual inspection makes picture books ideal for the two-year-old, and she will now even be able to sit with one and turn the pages one at a time, all on her own.

You may notice that she tries to translate the unfamiliar into the familiar. She may see a picture of a horse and call it a cat, if she is familiar with cats but no other animal. Help her understand the differences if she seems able to catch on, but don't push it. In these months she is learning so much that is new! Your role does not always have to be one of teacher. Accept your child's limitations and enjoy with her what she is able to enjoy in that moment. Her abilities will grow as she does.

Baby Animals by Gyo Fujikawa. Grosset and Dunlap, 1963. $3.95. This laminated board book introduces all of a baby's favorite little animals, with the corresponding sounds just right for learning to imitate.

The B Book by Stan and Jan Berenstain. Random House, 1971. $3.95. Here are thirty-three different words, all beginning with the letter *B,* and the Berenstains have written funny tales around them all.

Big Bad Bruce by Bill Peet. Houghton Mifflin, 1978. $11.95. Bruce, a bully of a bear, nearly tangles with a crafty old witch and changes his ways. What is appealing about Bruce is what is appealing about all of Peet's animal stories—the use of rhyme and rhythm in the telling, the bold and splashy cartoon-inspired illustrations, and the portrayal of animals more real than many human counterparts, with humanlike foibles and faults. A testament to Peet's endearing style comes from eighteen-month-old Amanda's parents in northeastern Massachusetts. Peet-lovers themselves, the parents had begun reading these stories to Amanda from infancy. One night, while her father was tucking her into bed, Amanda said to him, "Good night, you big bumbling brute"—a line straight out of *Big Bad Bruce.* Undaunted, her father continued to keep Amanda supplied with Peet stories. Skipping lightly over the text on another occasion, he misread, " ' "Har, har, hee, hee, ho, ho," chuckled Bruce.' " "No, Daddy," Amanda corrected, "chortled." The father, startled, looked down, and sure enough, Bruce indeed chortled. He never took license with Peet's language in Amanda's presence again. Also, *Cyrus, The Unsinkable Sea Serpent; The Pinkish, Purplish, Bluish Egg;* and *The Whingding-dilly.*

Brown Bear, Brown Bear, What Do You See? by Bill Martin, Jr., pictures by Eric Carle. Holt, Rinehart & Winston, 1983. $10.95. A trail of animals gives answers to the question asked in the title, from yellow duck to blue horse to green frog. At last the story turns to the reader and asks what he sees. Then watch for the responses to come tumbling out as your child proudly identifies all the colorful animals he's seen in the pages of this book.

Buster's Morning and **Buster's Afternoon** by Rod Campbell. Bedrick/Blackie, 1984. $5.95 each. In these two lift-the-flap books, Buster, a round-faced toddler in a blue stretchie, has fun uncovering objects and animals. Toddlers are often fascinated by things hidden away from them—hence the appeal in general of lift-the-flap books. But these are particularly good, because they reveal everyday objects, what your child might find if he really could open the washer, the cupboard, the birdhouse door, and so on.

Chubby Bear's Picnic by Yasuko Ito. Simon & Schuster, 1983. $2.95. Another book that can be read on both sides around, so to speak, because of its accordion-folded pages, this is panoramic in style. The text is small, but descriptive, and the softly colored pictures present a change of pace from the frequently bold and vivid colors of other books for the toddler set.

The Country Noisy Book by Margaret Wise Brown. Harper & Row, 1940. $8.95 hardcover, $1.95 paperback. Encourages active participation in the re-creation of the noises a little dog named Muffins hears when he goes to the country for the first time. A companion book is *The Indoor Noisy Book*.

Crash! Bang! Boom! by Peter Spier. Doubleday, 1972. $6.95. Each page is packed with pictures, identifying activities by their sounds, rather than by their names. A picture of pancakes being flipped reads "flop, flop." "Splatter, splatter" is—what else—an egg frying. And there are all kinds of bells, chiming, clanging, pinging, tinkling. It's all ended with rousing fireworks and booming cannons.

Cuddle Shape books. Random House, 1984. $3.95 each. This series of board books has many titles, but three worth noting are *Where Are All the Kittens?* by Jennifer Perryman, illustrated by Jan Brett; *The Care Bears' Circus of Shapes* by Peggy Kahn, illustrated by Carolyn Bracken; and *The Chipmunks' Counting Book* by Rochelle Blum. Designed to introduce the toddler to early concepts, these are enjoyable primarily for the friendly illustrations, familiar characters, and easy-to-manipulate board pages.

Cyndy Szekeres' Counting Book. Western Publishing, 1984. $2.95. A Golden Sturdy Shape Book. Peopled with mice, this takes a two-page spread for each number to be counted, so it's ideal for toddlers who like to look at big pictures, and yet it has enough detail to keep the child interested for more than a few seconds. Mice are walking, running, dancing, tickling, and gradually growing more and more tired, until at last we see ten mice sleeping. "Good night, mice." Happy counting for all.

Dancing in the Moon: Counting Rhymes by Fritz Eichenberg. Harcourt Brace Jovanovich, 1955. $12.95 hardcover, $1.95 paperback. "1 raccoon dancing in the moon," "2 moose scaring a papoose." Count from one to twenty in nonsense rhymes with vivid pictures giving full vent to the hilarious scenarios. The rhymes and the art are great for their own sakes, but they'll also be a great start for beginners learning their numbers.

Dr. Seuss's ABC. Random House, 1963. $4.95. "Big A, little a, what begins with A?" If you have any doubt that an alphabet book can be inventive, funny, and jolly reading, you haven't read *Dr. Seuss's ABC*. The rhymes are ear-catching, and they mix just the right amount of reality with nonsense. The pictures are classic Seuss in the hallmark style every parent and child will recognize.

The Duck Waddles by Elizabeth Wood. Random House, 1984. $1.95. Where does the duck go? Under, over, up, out, past, and so forth. Read the book on both sides—its accordion folds allow read-around capabilities. And follow the duck to a conceptual learning adventure. Other "read-arounds" are *The Cat Walks, The Rabbit Runs, The Frog Jumps,* and *The Puppy Races.*

Each Peach Pear Plum by Janet and Allan Ahlberg. Viking Kestrel, 1979. $10.95. An "I Spy" rhyme book, in which nursery-rhyme characters are hidden in the drawings. The rhyme will catch even younger ages than this, but once they reach the point-and-say stage, and also know their nursery-rhyme people, this book will become an even greater favorite. The art is so rich, so detailed, and so inviting that it's a must for every home library.

Early Words by Richard Scarry. Random House, 1976. $3.50. In this board book Frannie Bunny names household objects, rooms, and the people babies find there, like Daddy!

Flap Books by H. A. Rey. Houghton Mifflin. $1.75 each. **Anybody at Home?** (1942); **Feed the Animals** (1944); **See the Circus** (1956); and **Where's My Baby?** (1943). These lift-the-flap books work on the premise that each picture contains a secret:

Open the flap and the secret is shown. Toddlers reaching the secret-loving stage (secret games as well as telling secrets and, of course, hiding) won't be able to resist these paperbacks. They are small enough to hold and brightly colored enough to keep interest high.

Good Morning, Chick by Mirra Ginsburg, illustrated by Byron Barton. Greenwillow, 1980. $10.95. The easy to look at and brightly colored illustrations in this picture book emphasize a newborn chick's barnyard experiences, analogous to any toddler's. Here the chick returns to its mother's side, and comforting safety, after venturing out to see its new surroundings. The repetition of "like this" will make it a story your toddler will soon begin to chorus along with.

A House Is a House for Me by Mary Ann Hoberman, illustrated by Betty Fraser. Viking Kestrel, 1978. $7.95. Here is a wonderfully rhythmic tale with repetitive lines that kids will be singing along with as the story goes on. What's more, the book is big (more than eight inches by eleven inches), and the pages are packed with pictures of all the houses mentioned. "A web is a house for a spider/A bird builds its nest in a tree./There is nothing so snug as a bug in a rug/And a house is a house for me." What kind of house is a house for the "me" here? All kinds—boxes and trees and under a table and under an umbrella. The fun of the many hiding, snuggling, pretending places kids dream up is captured in this book.

I Unpacked My Grandmother's Trunk by Susan Ramsay Hoguet. Dutton, 1983. $10.95. I unpacked my grandmother's trunk . . . and look at the findings! Here, in an alphabet adventure and word game combination, there is treasure indeed. Half pages alternate with full pages to keep the previous sequence visible while the scene is changing, and the technique does much to keep the book alive with action. An acrobat is joined by a bear, then a cloud, then a dinosaur. And they don't sit still. It's fascinating to watch what pops up from the drawers in the old-fashioned trunk and see how the newcomer is greeted by the others. The bear, for example, delightfully silly, spies the igloo and crawls into it, which then begins to melt until it is so small, it only fits his head. By the time the windmill appears on the scene, it blows the dripping bear dry.

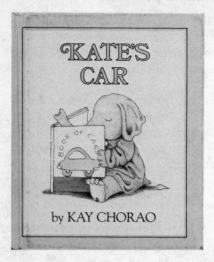

KATE'S CAR

BOOK OF CARS

by KAY CHORAO

Kate's Car by Kay Chorao. Dutton, 1982. $3.95. An elephant child cries "car," and her family misinterprets her meaning. The toddler will appreciate the little elephant's forlorn feeling, because it so wonderfully mirrors a child's own common experience of struggling to express desires in a limited way.

Max's First Words by Rosemary Wells. Dial, 1979. $3.50. A Dial Very First Book. This book shows familiar objects through the story of sister Ruby, who insists that baby Max say the words she wants him to say. Baby Max only wants to say "Bang!" Toddlers will appreciate Max's word choice and will love repeating it as he does. The surprise comes for the reader at the end when Ruby at last gives up and Max responds with "Delicious." Fine artwork makes it a pleasure for parents to buy and for children to look at. Also, *Max's New Suit, Max's Ride,* and *Max's Toys.*

Mr. Gumpy's Motor Car by John Burningham. T. Y. Crowell, 1976. $10.95 hardcover, $1.95 paperback. A menagerie of animals and a couple of children invite themselves along for a ride with Mr. Gumpy. But when the car gets stuck in the mud, will anyone help push? Teamwork is the only way to save the day in this delightful story with Burningham's scratchily painted pictures capturing the mood of the afternoon. Also, *Mr. Gumpy's Outing.*

Mouse House Days of the Week, illustrated by Helen Craig. Random House, 1983. $2.95. A very small accordion-fold book opens to show and teach the toddler the names of the days of the week.

My First Picture Dictionary by Katherine Howard, pictures by Huck Scarry. Random House, 1978. $1.50. Five hundred words and 250 pictures in this Pictureback® (a paperback picture book) make a good first dictionary indeed. Each picture is described in one simple line that should prompt toddlers to ask questions aplenty, while satisfying their intitial curiosity. But even younger babies will just love looking at all the pictures shown here and learning the names. A good step-up book—enjoy it first for the pictures themselves and use it for a reference later on.

My Shirt Is White by Dick Bruna. Methuen, 1972. We name the colors as a girl gets dressed in her "underneath" clothes and her outerwear. Simple line drawings, the hallmark of the Bruna style, really come across to toddlers. No longer available for sale, it can still be found in many library collections. And, of course, Dick Bruna's numerous other books for toddlers are in many stores. They deal with concepts such as letters, numbers, and prepositions (in, on, under), all in the same simply delineated style of art.

Noisy Nora by Rosemary Wells. Dial, 1973. $9.95 hardcover, $3.95 paperback. Wonderful rhyme combines with crosshatch pen and color illustrations to spin the tale of the middle child of a mouse family who must wait for some attention. To get her demands, Nora's tactic is to make noise. But she soon discovers that she gets more notice when she leaves the house in utter, startling quiet.

Numbers by Jan Piénkowski. Simon & Schuster, 1974. $4.95. This is a very good early counting book, because the pictures are clear, simply outlining forms of the different items to be counted. Brightly colored, they are attractive to the toddler's eye. One leopard, four ducks, ten apples—your child will feel very satisfied at being able to identify and tell how many of each of these flowers, fruits, animals, and people she sees.

Nutcracker by E.T.A. Hoffman, pictures by Maurice Sendak. Crown, 1984. $19.95. This unusually handsome volume is meant for home libraries, for display, and for reading to children of all ages. Sendak has created magical illustrations that bring the quintessential holiday tale to life.

Once Upon a Potty by Alona Frankel. Barron's, 1980. $3.95. A helpful title that parents can use with ready-for-toilet-training toddlers, this is now available in his and hers editions to make it a particularly personal choice.

Our Animal Friends at Maple Hill Farm by Alice and Martin Provensen. Random House, 1974. $9.95. At Maple Hill Farm one has the pleasure not only of meeting all the animal inhabitants, but also of finding out lots about their ways, their likes and dislikes, how they do things, what they eat, where they sleep, and much, much more. This is a large book (more than eight inches by eleven inches), and each page has different subjects—it might have whimsical pictures of the chickens and tell what their names are, or tell a bit about the cats there and what they like to do. But no matter what, each page is filled with something as funny as the previous one, until by the end one is filled with the riotous sense of life teeming at Maple Hill Farm.

Pooh's Counting Book by A. A. Milne, illustrated by E. H. Shepard. Dutton, 1983. $4.95. Who wouldn't want to give their child an introduction to counting conducted by Pooh and friends? This little volume will actually be more useful just for the fun of learning the names of numbers by hearing them as Milne used them in his writings. What is included are quotations and drawings from *Winnie-the-Pooh*, *The House at Pooh Corner*, and *Now We Are Six* that contain numbers. A neat idea.

The Pudgy Pat-a-Cake Book, illustrated by Terri Super. Grosset and Dunlap, 1983. $2.95. A die-cut board book filled with rhymes and finger-and-toe games, illustrated with pandas, puppies, bunnies, and kittens. Parents can use it as a prompter to get children started thinking about games they might like to make up themselves.

Putt-Putt Board Books. The Little Red Car, The Noisy Green Engine, The Big Blue Truck, The Busy Orange Tractor, and **The Sturdy Yellow Tugboat.** Simon & Schuster, 1984. $2.95 each. The vehicle in the title is the main character of each of these, and young toddlers will love imitating all the fascinating sounds that the vehicles make or that occur when this vehicle is around. Considerable imagination has been used to create the noises—" 'Chuff chuff,' the little green engine chugs up a hill.'' Older toddlers will soon begin pretending they are the vehicle.

The Runaway Bunny by Margaret Wise Brown, pictures by Clement Hurd. Harper & Row, 1972. $7.95 hardcover, $2.95 paperback. A little bunny asserts his independence by running away, but Mother rightly assures him she will be right behind to find him. The mother's echoing of her son's statements rings out so strongly with positive reinforcement that you feel all the mother's love overcoming all the child's resistance.

Sam books by Barbro Lindgren, illustrated by Eva Eriksson. William Morrow, 1982, 1983. $5.00 to $6.25. **Sam's Ball, Sam's Bath, Sam's Car, Sam's Cookie, Sam's Lamp,** and **Sam's Teddy Bear.** What the toddler Sam does with all his possessions is likely to mirror your own toddler's activities as he begins to develop a sense of imagination. For example, in *Sam's Bath* we see the little boy trying to give his dog a bath at the same time as his tub is filled with all his other possessions. He takes on the imitative role of adult, something you're likely to see your own child doing. The sheer fun of bathtime is exuberantly rendered.

Shh! Bang! by Margaret Wise Brown, pictures by Robert Veyrac. Harper & Row, 1942. Billed as ''A Whispering Book,'' this is written to be both whispered and spoken out loud when read to the toddler, who will love imitating the whisper-words (printed in teeny tiny print) and the out-loud words. The story of a boy who finds a town where everyone whispers and decides to wake them up holds up in spite of

SAM'S BATH
Barbro Lindgren
illustrated by Eva Eriksson

its dated-looking art. No longer available for sale—look for it in library collections.

Shopping Trip by Helen Oxenbury. Simon & Schuster, 1982. $3.50. Though Oxenbury has done several other wordless picture books, this remains one of the best and also easiest to follow, as we see the youngster on an outing and "read" of the adventures that occur.

The Sleepytime Book by Margaret Hillert, illustrated by Rod Ruth. Western Publishing, 1975. $4.95. A small spiral-bound book with flaps to lift, it pictures tiny little animals going to sleep. It's just right for toddlers who will be encouraged to imitate these drowsy baby creatures.

The Story About Ping by Marjorie Flack, illustrated by Kurt Wiese. Viking Kestrel, 1933. $10.95 hardcover, $3.50 paperback.

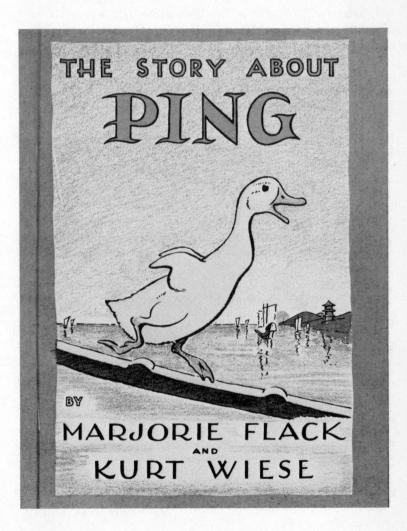

This classic tale is of one little duckling who did not want to be last and get the requisite spanking, and so hid from his family and was nearly caught for supper. The wonderful lilting rhythmic prose is a pleasure to read aloud, and most one- to six-year-olds should appreciate both the sound and sense of the story as well as the line illustrations of Kurt Wiese.

Strawberry Shortcake's Bathtime Book by Carolyn Bracken. Random House, 1984. $2.50. Shows Strawberry Shortcake as she bathes, dresses, and ties up a package for Lime Chiffon's birthday. Made of soft, nontoxic vinyl.

A Surprise for Max by Hanne Turk. Neugebauer Press, Picture Book Studio, 1982. $3.50. Max the mouse finds a wrapped package waiting for him, and he wrestles with it until he has the satisfaction—as does the toddler following his story—of discovering the treasure: a toy cat on a pull string.

Teddy Bear Postman by Phoebe, Selby, and Joan Worthington. Frederick Warne, 1982. $6.95. Teddy Bear Postman has a special mission on Christmas Eve. British in flavor, but not inaccessible, this is a sweet lap-size book that children with a fondness for teddy bears are sure to love. Also by the authors: *Teddy Bear Gardener* and *Teddy Bear Baker*.

A Tiny Word Book by Gyo Fujikawa. Grosset and Dunlap, 1968. $2.25. From seashore to garden to jungle, people, creatures of nature, articles of clothing, and other things in many settings are named. Swan, pear, plant, tree—simple, delightful, tiny pictures are just right for an eighteen-month-old, who will find this a wonderful "source-book" to turn to over and over again, to name the pictures as she learns to speak.

What Do You See? by Janina Domanska. Macmillan, 1974. $9.95. Some whimsical, lushly colored animals look at the world only from one perspective, but a high-flying lark sees all the world's beauty. Good for teaching concepts, this book will be well used to ask the child what he sees as he begins to build the notion that things can be viewed in many different ways—for color, for texture, and from above, below, or far away.

Where the Wild Things Are by Maurice Sendak. Harper & Row, 1963. $10.89 hardcover, $4.95 paperback. A Caldecott Medal Winner. One night, Max acts beastly to his mother and becomes a king of the wild things, who "roared their terrible roars and gnashed their terrible teeth." But even as king he is lonely and wants to be where someone loves him best of all, and so he sails home again to find his supper waiting. The power of this story comes through in Sendak's masterly illustrations, sophisticated and yet appealing to children. A work of art, it speaks to the essence of every child's fantasies and fears.

Chapter Five

FROM TWO TO THREE YEARS

*W*hile the third year of life has been nicknamed the terrible twos, you will soon learn firsthand that this characterization is somewhat less than true. This year will probably hold just as many pleasant and tranquil days for your toddler and you as it will days of anger, temper tantrums, and tears. When you see good days, it is because the two-year-old is testing and discovering her abilities with success. However, when she becomes frustrated by her inability to achieve what she wants or to communicate her desire, watch out. Not yet able to understand what is possible and what is not, two-year-olds find the impossible an unpleasant surprise. And that may bring on the tempest.

When she reached the age of twenty-four months, the two-year-old was safe and secure. As she begins to grow and develop new capabilities, she enters a period of uncertainty. The world may seem large and confusing to the toddler who is now noticing more and more, thanks to her new powers of observation, her increased mobility, and her improving language skills, all of which enable her to request—sometimes demand—and be given more information. Because she is uncertain, she responds to the world by trying to assert some control over her life, to once again set things right according to her viewpoint. Parents of a two-year-old quickly learn that the routines or rituals their child establishes are not to be ignored. The two-year-old needs to be able to count on the familiar, and *again* or *more* may seem to be her favorite word right now.

Next to those a two-year-old's favorite word is likely *mine*. The two- to three-year-old is full of egocentrism. As she participates in parallel play and eventually interacts with other toddlers, her aggressiveness and need to dominate playthings will be apparent. There is no cause for alarm. At this stage your child will seem unable to view things—both objects and situations—from any viewpoint but her own. The flip side of that coin is that she also assumes all objects, animals, and natural phenomena have the same qualities of life she does. She lives, cries, feels happy or sad, and so do her favorite toy, the apple tree outside, clouds, the sun, and so forth. Your toddler is not yet exercising an imagination, though she truly believes the door that is slammed too hard may hurt and be sad. She places everything under the same limited rules of order by which she lives. And because she wants to control things, she may have a sense of almost godlike power about herself. The child who performs elaborate magic rituals to "keep the sky blue" or "help the sun to shine" is exercising a natural inclination toward superstition common at this stage of development. Here is found the precursor to empathic feeling and the capacity for make-believe, both of which will be seen at a later stage.

Visually the two-year-old shows an increased awareness of objects farther away from her. As she is beginning to be able to concentrate on one thing and still remain aware of another nearby, her peripheral vision is developing now to aid her too. Physical developments, aside from growth, include a greater deftness of fine motor skills, allowing her to manipulate large puzzle pieces, to work simple puzzles, to use paintbrushes or crayons, or to mold clay.

The concepts a two-year-old is learning to master are still limited, but she is now gaining a sense of time—determined by events, however, and not by the clock. Because of her routines and developing memory, if you ask her in the afternoon what she did in the morning, she will know that she woke up, got dressed, and had breakfast. She has an increased interest in her past history now, too, and delights in hearing over and over about her babyhood and the things she did as an infant. Her skill at grouping and association is also developing as she defines her own sense of appropriateness. Now like must always go with like, and opposites are to be separated. A big daddy pretending to put on a little baby's sweater may be violently opposed by your toddler: This is no joke—it's unacceptable behavior, from your two-year-old's point of view.

Language acquisition varies greatly from child to child at this point. For some it is the time of flowering speech and greater interest in conversation. As long as your child's understanding is coming along, don't worry about actual speech—it will follow in time. Continue to encourage language acquisition, however, because what he understands now forms the basis for his verbal skills whenever they do begin to blossom. And if he is an early bloomer, he is to be encouraged to continue developing.

You can prompt interaction by asking questions, or by elaborating on what the child himself states. If he has a ball in his hands and says, "See ball," you can follow up on that by saying, "Yes, I see the ball. That is a red ball. It is round," or giving other facts about the ball. He will eventually learn all about balls, of course, and be able to assess in one glance, without thinking, that he sees a round red ball—but he is just starting to learn all that now, just as some months ago he had to test physical properties over and over to learn those too. Stick to what is at hand, and let his own interests be your guide.

Talk to your two-year-old about only one topic at a time, especially if it's one he's brought up himself, and you will soon see how enjoyable and satisfying such an exchange can be. Later you can move from one topic to another, but this is likely to be too confusing for a child at this age.

Remember, too, that a two- to three-year-old doesn't listen to words only for meaning. To him words are music, and their sounds and the sounds of sentences have a fascinating rhythm, much like the music he is discovering he likes to sing and march to. As with music, he likes words that have a good *strong* sound in themselves and in combination with others. Prose with a rhythm and beat, and a refrain that will become familiar and dear, will be as popular as rhyme itself. He will be heard repeating snatches of tunes or words from a familiar rhyme or jingle as he plays, or he may make the verbal sound effects of objects that he particularly likes, such as clanging bells, cars revving up, horns honking. He loves these sounds for themselves and also, as we will see in the next stage of development, because they are beginning to extend the meaning of his play.

What are some of the better choices for a two-year-old's books?

Generally speaking, books that use photographs for illustration are fascinating now, because the two-year-old likes to see things as they really look. Give him books that depict concepts as he begins to master certain ones, such as around, under, and the differences between big and little. (He'll begin to be very certain about those!) And for youngsters with their firm routines, books abound that show similar wake-up, daily, and bedtime rituals being performed by other little children in other households. Your child will be sure to tell you if that is how he gets ready for bed. Books that are not really fantasies but do possess an understanding of your two-year-old's often intense attachment to inanimate objects, or empathy for things of nature, are also likely to keep his attention.

Animal Builders, Animal Climbers, Animal Jumpers, Animal Runners, and **Animal Swimmers** by Kenneth Lilly. Random House, 1984. $2.95 each. One-line-per-page text is distinguished

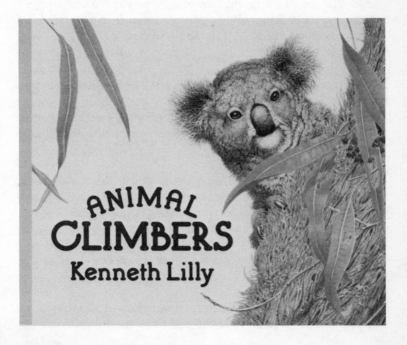

by beautiful artwork, excellent for children who have become fascinated by animals—although some species mentioned are exotic, so parents who use these books with their children and want to expand on the text should be prepared to do some digging for their own information first.

Baby Bear's Bedtime and **Good Morning, Baby Bear** by Eric Hill. Random House, 1983. $3.95 each. The creator of Spot (see page 37) brings us a lovable little bear who's quite set in his bedtime and early morning routines. Though simple, this is an unusually reassuring and cozy book. Single parents should note that here only Mother and Baby Bear seem to make up the family, and the books make that seem as warm a unit as any.

Blackboard Bear by Martha Alexander. Dial, 1969. $6.50. Left on his own, a little brother dreams up a playmate and becomes the envy of the older kids. The book captures a youngster's feelings of solitude and deals with the sometimes scary feeling of wanting revenge. Blackboard Bear is the kind of imaginary friend who will give readers a sense of power. When he steps down from the chalkboard and into the book, the child feels well protected. Also, *We're in Big Trouble, Blackboard Bear*.

The Carrot Seed by Ruth Krauss, pictures by Crockett Johnson. Harper & Row, 1945. $7.89. A little boy has faith, in spite of his family's doubts, that his carrot seed will grow. A surefire reinforcement story for the frustrating times in a two-year-old's life, it shows that patience is rewarded.

Emma by Wendy Kesselman, illustrated by Barbara Cooney. Doubleday, 1980. $9.95. Based on a true story, this tells of a grandmother in her seventies who takes up painting in order to have a picture of her hometown as she knew it. In this sweet and warm book the Caldecott Medal–winning Cooney has captured the depth of Emma's artistic life. Emma's determination and her growth from loneliness to self-pride and fulfillment will appeal to sympathetic toddlers.

Freight Train by Donald Crews. Greenwillow, 1978. $9.75. (A 1985 paperback edition is scheduled.) Graphically designed, this picture book uses colors with black-and-white for effective power. The text describes in bold statements the majesty of the freight train, which has fascinated kids (and their parents) since its introduction. The speed, the force, the rush and roar of the train, all culminate in an exciting finish to a spectacular book. A *wow* eye-opener for toddlers, this will excite parents too.

The Guessing Game by Betsy and Giulio Maestro. Grosset and Dunlap, 1983. $3.50. A youngster's version of twenty questions has Emily Pig looking for something, and her animal friends try to figure out what it is from the clues she gives them. The fun is more the game than the surprise, because kids will try to guess along with the characters.

Halloween Surprises by Ann Schweninger. Viking Kestrel, 1984. $9.95. A companion to *Christmas Secrets*, this story takes the rabbit family Brown on trick-or-treating adventures. Dialogue in balloons gives a sense of immediacy to all that is going on and will let little ones really get into the characters as they get involved with the surprises found by the rabbit children on Halloween.

The Harbor by Philippe Dupasquier. Grosset and Dunlap, 1984. $3.95. A Busy Places Book. Young children are often fascinated with catastrophes. Here is a lively story, the pages of the book teeming with the action that takes place at harborside. Suddenly Captain Jack's boat is sinking. "Poor Captain Jack," says Joe—words that are echoed by young Jenny, her father reports, for she loves to repeat that heartfelt phrase and other lines from the book every time her father reads it to her, especially the last line—"And don't be late."

Homes by Jan Piénkowski. Simon & Schuster, 1977. $4.95. What could be more basic to a small child's sense of territoriality than the word *home*? Piénkowski's varied-color artwork, in simple, almost childlike outline style, introduces youngsters to many kinds of homes: doghouse, stable, web, and others.

I Can Count by Dick Bruna. Methuen, 1968. $2.50. Two hair bows, four spoons, five rabbits—all easy to see in the classic, simple Bruna tradition, so that two-year-olds will quickly catch on to the fun of counting them up and will be so pleased with this accomplishment!

an I CAN DO IT ALL BY MYSELF book

I'm the king of the castle!

Story by Shigeo Watanabe   Pictures by Yasuo Ohtomo

PLAYING ALONE

I Can Do It All by Myself books by Shigeo Watanabe and Yasuo Ohtomo. Philomel, 1980–1982. $8.95 hardcover, $3.95 paperback. Individual titles: **How Do I Put It On?, What a Good Lunch!, Get Set! Go!,** and **I'm the King of the Castle!** In some, particularly the first, Bear's accomplishments are exactly akin to any two- to three-year-old's. But in any case, his feeling of pride in his abilities is something toddlers at this age will really enjoy. And all are encouragement to imitate Bear's striving. Other titles in the series: *I Can Ride It, I Can Build a House.*

I Can Read by Dick Bruna. Methuen, 1965. $2.50. The device is simple but to the point: A child points at and names different body parts in each picture frame, something two-year-olds should be able to do along with her. To that, add the written word on the page, and you've got a child "reading," but no matter—he or she will find the named object Bruna has cleverly colored in, so the accomplishment is there either way.

I Know a Lot of Things by Ann and Paul Rand. Harcourt Brace Jovanovich, 1956. $1.35 paperback. A creative and refreshing book with art that looks at times like paper cutouts, at times like the splashes of a toddler, but always adds an extra dimension to this look at the world from a child's perspective. It sees all of what a child sees in things, not just one aspect or another, and manages to convey in single sentences facts and fancies, accomplishments and wonderments, what is attainable by a child, and what will expand his world. "I know I can wave hello to a mushroom who's just a little fellow with a big umbrella." Just a sample—read this one for yourself and with your child; it will give you a new insight into how he sees all that he sees.

In & Out, Up & Down. A Sesame Street® Chunky Board Book. Random House, 1982. $2.95. Muppet characters show opposites like *in* the tub and *out* of the tub. A square book that floats, it is easy for little hands to hold.

Just Cats: Six Learning Groups by John Burningham. Viking Kestrel, 1983. $4.95. Children will learn to group things together when following the story of one cat who sets off to have a picnic, carrying a huge basket. Along the way he is joined by other cats, who encounter and outwit other animals until they can enjoy the surprise inside—a birthday cake. The book folds out, with flaps for lifting. It is one of a series called Number Play books, which includes *Read One*, in which you lift the flaps to see the bears and read the numbers one through five, and *Pigs Plus*, which teaches simple number combinations and arithmetic through a story, for older children. A pig sets off for a ride in an old red car only to meet a succession of difficulties, as well as other pigs, who are to be added until five pigs get the car going again. Also, *Count Up* and *Five Down*.

Just Like Daddy by Frank Asch. Prentice-Hall, 1981. $10.95 hardcover, $4.95 paperback. Repeated phrase of the title will be sung out by two-year-olds with each successive reading of this book, which shows a young child imitating Daddy. Strikes a warm, friendly mood that makes the book particularly inviting.

Leonardo da Vinci by Alice and Martin Provensen. Viking Kestrel, 1984. $14.95. A brilliant pop-up book, its three-dimensional, movable pictures fascinate even children who are much too young to understand the book's subject. Its sturdy engineering makes it appropriate for youngsters (it is fairly hardy for a pop-up book), and adults will be amazed at how wonderfully da Vinci's discoveries are displayed. Alice and Martin Provensen, Caldecott Medal–winning illustrators, have done exquisite artistic justice to the life and milieu of the genius.

Let's Look Books by Bill Gillham and Susan Hulm, photos by Jan Siegieda. Putnam's, 1984. $4.95 each. **Let's Look at Colors, Let's Look at Numbers, Let's Look at Opposites,** and **Let's Look at Shapes**. Photographs are used to show colors, numbers, opposites, and shapes in four separate titles, in full-color that will catch the eyes of toddlers and keep them looking as the parent or other adult reviews with them the words and pictures and ideas presented here.

A Little Alphabet by Trina Schart Hyman. Little, Brown, 1980. $4.95. One lovely letter per page, embroidered with details—the letter *g* alone holds a girl, a goose, a geranium, a gnome, grapes, and grass. See what you and your children can name. The helpful author has provided a list in the back of the book to tell you what you've missed, but no fair peeking.

Little Books by John Burningham. T. Y. Crowell, 1975, 1976. $3.95 each, except **The Rabbit**, $2.50. **The Blanket, The Cupboard, The Dog, The School, The Snow,** and **The Friend**. All of these simple storybooks make good follow-ups to earlier board books, because here a simple event or situation in a very real little child's life (a lost blanket must be recovered, a pet rabbit caught before it eats Dad's garden) is the focus, rather than merely the objects or people.

The Little House by Virginia Lee Burton. Houghton Mifflin, 1942, 1969. $8.95 hardcover, $2.95 paperback. Once upon a time a little house in the country wondered what it would be like to live in the city. Eventually the city began to grow around her, and she grew old and shabby until the great-great-granddaughter of the man who had built the little house saw her and moved her back where she belonged. A Caldecott Medal winner, this book is a classic that captures the hearts of all who have ever wished life into their inanimate but beloved dwellings.

Little Toy Board Books by Rodney Peppé. Viking Kestrel, 1984. $2.95 each. **Little Wheels, Little Circus, Little Games, Little Numbers,** and **Little Dolls**. In these five board books little toys play imaginative games. You will enjoy naming them for your youngster, and later on your child will enjoy participating in or elaborating on the make-believe scenarios.

Look What I Can Do by Jose Aruego. Scribner's, 1971. $6.95 hardcover, $2.95 paperback. Red and yellow accent the action in this nearly wordless book that has two *carabaos* (imaginary creatures) in a game of one-upmanship stunts much like those you'll see two human children get involved in.

Madeline by Ludwig Bemelmans. Viking Kestrel, 1939. $11.95 hardcover, $3.50 paperback. This story about the twelve little girls, including the heroine, Madeline, who attend school in an enchantingly sketched Paris, is a childhood classic. A former bookseller recalls listening in on a conversation between a daughter and her parents browsing in the children's section and their reaction to *Madeline*: "Mom, Dad, look who I've found," exclaimed the young woman, who appeared to be around eighteen and a college freshman. "It's

Madeline!'' The discovery was like finding a long-lost best friend, and they couldn't lose her again, so they bought a copy to keep her with them forever. If you love *Madeline,* you'll want to try *Madeline's Rescue* and *Madeline and the Bad Hat.*

Moja Means One by Muriel Feelings, pictures by Tom Feelings. Dial, 1972. $2.25 paperback. A Swahili counting book illustrated with facets of African life that is sure to expand a child's world. The award-winning art truly brings us into another way of life in an engaging manner.

Moonlight and **Sunshine** by Jan Ormerod. Lothrop, Lee & Shepard, 1981 and 1982. $8.95 each. Wordless picture books that show the awakening and retiring of a family on a typical day. What makes them noteworthy is the quality of the representation: the feelings that come through; all the subtleties of the relationships of mother, father, and daughter; and the wonderful light and color that fill this household and play upon the faces of the three people shown.

My Good Morning Book by Eloise Wilkin. A Golden Sturdy Shape Book. Western Publishing, 1983. $2.95. A child learning to dress and feed himself will appreciate the simple joys found here—as a boy awakens and gets a piggyback ride downstairs from Daddy and a "Good morning!" from Mom. Here is also a reassuring, close-knit family scene. Similar, with a female protagonist, is *My Goodnight Book*.

My Very First Library. T. Y. Crowell, 1974. $3.95 each. **My Very First Book of Colors, My Very First Book of Numbers, My Very First Book of Shapes,** and **My Very First Book of Words.** Four spiral-bound board books with pages split sideways, each book is geared to teaching matching concepts.

Noisy Words by John Burningham. Viking Kestrel, 1984. $4.95 each. **Wobble Pop, Skip Trip,** and **Sniff Shout**. Three board books depict scenes that show a child's daily activities—playing, cleaning, meeting friends—and the words that go along with each. The difference between these and some of the similar books for a younger age is that here the child's day moves in a sequence, to enable you or your child to put a story together from all the scenes as each weaves into the next.

The Other Bone by Ed Young. Harper & Row, 1984. $9.95. A wordless picture book showing a dog that mistakes one bone for two after seeing the reflection of the one in a pool. Children will appreciate the predicament.

Over, Under, and Through by Tana Hoban. Macmillan, 1973. $10.95. In photographs children in various activities illustrate twelve spatial concepts (a chick is *on* a hand, a letter goes *in* a mailbox)— including around, across, between, beside, below, against, behind. Look at these for their photographic detail as well as for the lesson in concepts.

Peterkin Meets a Star by Emilie Boon. Random House, 1984. $4.95. Peterkin picks a star from the sky, but the star is sad, so Peterkin puts it back into the sky, where it watches over him all night. Perfect for the two-year-old's interest in stories with anthropomorphism.

Peterkin's Wet Walk by Emilie Boon. Random House, 1984. $4.95. In this story a mushroom shelters Peterkin and his friends as it becomes an umbrella, then a boat, and leads them to a deer, who gives them all a ride home. Thanking the deer and the mushroom, Peterkin and friends go in to supper. The beautiful colors in this book seem almost luminescent, and the fantasy is quite in tune with a two-year-old's belief that he can command the elements.

The Rain Puddle by Adelaide Hall, illustrated by Roger Duvoisin. Lothrop, Lee & Shepard, 1965. $10.80. Like *The Other Bone,* this book treats the concept of reflections through an anthropomorphic story—here barnyard animals seem to be drowning, but of course they remain safe and sound.

Richard Scarry's Best First Book Ever! Random House, 1979. $4.95. A cast of cheery-looking animal characters make learning words, numbers, colors, shapes, and even manners exactly the kind of fun it ought to be.

The Rose in My Garden by Anita Lobel, illustrated by Arnold Lobel. Greenwillow, 1984. $11.50. A cumulative tale in the style of ''The House That Jack Built,'' this begins in the garden with a rose on which a bee sleeps. The paintings are lush with hollyhocks, zinnias, marigolds, and sunflowers, and are cumulative complements to the verse text. Recommended for concept building as well as for the delight of the verse and art.

Rosie's Walk by Pat Hutchins. Macmillan, 1968. $10.95 hardcover, $3.95 paperback. Rosie, a hen, is out for a walk. The fox is on her trail, but she doesn't seem to know it. Unwittingly she leads him into disaster, and we have the satisfaction of viewing his come-uppance. Mild suspense for the toddler, who will wait with bated breath to see if the fox will get the unsuspecting hen.

Round & Round & Round by Tana Hoban. Greenwillow, 1983. $9.00. Round wagon wheels, a basketball balancing on a seal's nose (an amusing picture as well as an instructive one!), peas in a bowl, a hamster on a treadmill—all show us wordlessly, in photos, so many round things. The book imparts a concept of the shape for the child, but parents will find that after many viewings it also continues to be impressive for its new perspective on what we take for granted as ordinary.

Round and Round the Garden by William Stobbs. The Bodley Head, 1982. $7.50. An interpretation of the well-loved tickling game, sure to appeal to any silly toddler, is made into a sweet story, with pictures to look at over and over as you play. ("Round and Round the Garden," for the uninitiated, consists of circling the child's palm with a finger, walking the finger slowly up the child's arm, then quickly tickling her under the arm.)

Sam Who Never Forgets by Eve Rice. Greenwillow, 1977. $10.95 hardcover, $3.95 Picture Puffin paperback. Rounded shapes show a zookeeper feeding all the animals, except Elephant, whose fears are allayed when he gets the biggest load of hay.

Seven Little Rabbits by John Becker, illustrated by Barbara Cooney. Walker, 1973. Scholastic paperback, 1984. $2.50. Award-winner Cooney has filled her Beatrix Potter–like paintings with delightful details, which only increase the charm of this tale. The story itself is a rhythmic counting story, a bedtime story about seven little rabbits walking down the road to call on old friend toad. It has rep-etition (just enough) to call for the involvement of children even younger than two, but the main thrust is likely to hit them just around the age where bedtime rituals and learning to count coincide.

Sizes by Jan Piénkowski. Simon & Schuster, 1973. $4.95. The opening pages of this book are delightful and give a taste of the fun to come: Graduating sizes of dolls with smiling faces greet the reader.

But the text is devoted to only two sizes—big and little. So we have big truck, little car; big airplane, little bird; big elephant, little mouse. All show relationships of a sort but really serve to emphasize a size difference and no other, which is fine for teaching that one concept.

Sleepytime Bunny by Stephen Cosgrove and Charles Reasoner. Price/Stern/Sloan, 1984. $2.50. In this board book a young rabbit's bedtime rituals take place in a cozy family situation. The art is notable for its appropriate details (a carrot quilt for Bunny). The text is notable in calling on readers to help Bunny out—find his bathtub duck and bedtime teddy. But most of all the story is notable because it shows how proud the young rabbit is of his accomplishments— putting on his pajamas and putting away his clothes. And these ideas combined make this a delight for two-year-olds.

The Snowman by Raymond Briggs. Random House, 1978. $4.95. In this wordless story filled with enchantment, a small boy builds a snowman on a wintry day and the snowman comes alive. Hazy, magical pictures capture the feeling of frosty-aired days and draw the reader into the fantasy.

Take Another Look by Tana Hoban. Greenwillow, 1981. $10.25. As your child progresses beyond the need to feel the textures as he learns the words that name them, try this remarkable book with him. A circle cut in every other page reveals parts of a black-and-white photograph. When you turn the page, you see the whole. So you get a close-up look and are treated to remarkable details of fur, flowers, sponges, a sandwich, a shell. See which are bumpy, smooth, soft, or hard, and also look at these objects as if seeing them for the very first time. A visual treat for adults as well as children.

Tan Tan's Suspenders and **Tan Tan's Hat** by Kazuo Iwamura. Bradbury Press, 1983. $7.95 each. Tan Tan's hat is for tossing up into the sky, rolling, and catching things. His suspenders also do a lot more than just hold up his pants. Both afford him a lot more fun than ordinarily, but then, Tan Tan is no ordinary monkey! Pictures correspond so exactly to text that this is a good first reading experience for older children as well.

Ten, Nine, Eight by Molly Bang. Greenwillow, 1983. $10.00. (A 1985 paperback edition is scheduled.) A book with many facets—here a black girl and her father count down to bedtime. Bang's Caldecott-honor art is expressive and warm, and should soothe any child into sleep.

There's a Nightmare in My Closet by Mercer Mayer. Dial, 1968. $3.50 paperback. A small boy conquers his fear of the dark by letting his nightmare (depicted as a big, ugly monster) out of the closet and shooting it with his popgun. Poor nightmare—the monster is really just a big baby who cries at being shot, so the boy has to tuck it into bed to comfort it. The story and art are combined with humor in treating a sensitive topic, so kids will easily be drawn into the situation.

Ton and Pon: Big and Little and **Ton and Pon: Two Good Friends** by Kazuo Iwamura. Bradbury Press, 1984. $8.95 each. In two separate tales, two dogs demonstrate the good qualities of their sizes. The cartoonlike illustrations can easily be "read" without the texts.

The Very Hungry Caterpillar by Eric Carle. Philomel, 1979. $9.95. The voracious appetite of this likable insect illustrates for children the themes of growing up and change as the caterpillar is transformed into a glorious butterfly.

We Hide, You Seek by Jose Aruego and Ariane Dewey. Greenwillow, 1979. $7.95. A clumsy rhino can't seem to find any of the animals camouflaged in their hiding places but startles the animals into revealing themselves anyway. This vibrant picture book not only captures the provocative notion of animals hiding but also uses animals of East Africa, identified in the endpapers, as characters, so the book has double value.

What Sadie Sang by Eve Rice. Greenwillow, 1983. $8.95. A toddler who doesn't want to walk is put in the stroller, and as she is strolled along she sings her special song. Illuminating an everyday experience, this is a wonderful book for sharing, because the adults who hear Sadie sing to the trees and the dogs and all whom she passes enjoy hearing her as much as do children Sadie's age.

Chapter Six
FROM THREE TO FOUR YEARS

*W*hen your child reaches the age of three, he may seem to be newly nimble-fingered, surefooted, and self-confident. He has mastered so much of what seemed to be difficult about his previous year. The baby who once had trouble balancing while trying to throw or catch a ball and seemed awkward fingering small objects now loves all those activities and more—hopping on one or two feet, skipping, running and stopping short at his own will, or just poking along at a slow walk while being absorbed in thinking or doing something else. Your three-year-old has probably even mastered the art of dressing himself, with the exception of troublesome hooks or buttons.

Visually he takes great interest in details and will exhibit that interest when you read with him. He understands and can point to the correct shape if you ask, ''What is round?'' ''What is square?'' He can identify colors as well. He can follow a moving target visually without losing his attention and can look from near to far and back again without confusion. But his particular interest right now is in looking at people and all the changes in their facial expressions.

The three-year-old's great accomplishments come in the areas of language acquisition and socialization. In this year your child will pick up all the vocabulary he needs to express his basic needs, desires, and questions. His reliance on gestures and noises to convey needs or feelings fades away—they become for him, as for the rest of us, a means of elaborating on the meaning of words.

Now he is able to speak in comparison—to identify which item is big, bigger, biggest. He uses plurals in speaking, and his sentences become more complete. No longer will he say, "Me go." He will say firmly, "I want to go." His speech reflects his understanding of relative location: In, on, under, over, between, and behind are now incorporated into his repertoire. He is able to focus in more narrowly when answering questions too. For example, the child of three who is asked where he sleeps may now respond, "In my room in my bed," quite location specific.

Because he can now contemplate the idea of choice without being confused or upset by the idea, he loves to be asked his preference, and words like *maybe, might,* and *could* are now wielded with power and relished. He can talk about time more conceptually, and although he still understands it with regard to activities, he knows there is a relationship between the object called a clock and the time when activities are performed. If he's waiting to do something, he may even pretend to tell time by looking at the clock and announcing, "It's late o'clock." His most frequently used time-words are for the future, though, rather than the past, and his chief interest in the past remains in himself in the past. He wants to distinguish himself from his former baby-self and will frequently ask, "Could I do this when I was a baby?" He means "Look at me. I'm a big boy now, not the baby I was." Acknowledge that you agree with him!

Some of the three-year-old's favorite words now express her love of surprises and secrets, and even the mention of those words may set her off in delight. She enjoys silly words, nonsense rhymes, and noises that delight the ear.

Her relationships with other children will show a dramatic change during the span from three to four. While she acknowledged other children before but did not interact with them (quite different from defending her objects or possessions from them), she now finds other children immensely interesting. She directs conversation to them, and friends become important. Cooperative behavior increases, and you will see a blossoming of flirtatious behavior between boys and girls. The object-oriented two-year-old has become the other-child-oriented three-year-old, and you're apt to find that this interest is expressed in often silly ways. Three-year-olds seem to love clowning around with each other for hours of amusement that even slightly older children (especially siblings of a few years older) and adults find ridiculous. A three-year-old's "joke" may be to spit or make faces or say things with no rhyme or reason to an adult, but they send her into peals of laughter. In fact, you will find that the three-year-old "sillies" often result in the child literally laughing until she cries.

By now the child is able to listen better (although sometimes she may act as if she doesn't hear you at all). She still loves songs, nursery rhymes, and stories, and can pay attention for as long as twenty minutes. Fantasy and symbolic play peak during this time. Children use play to practice the social rules they see adults enacting and to reconstruct them. Fantasy play also serves as a way to escape demands that seem to be a natural part of growing up. She may also enact the forbidden in make-believe play as a means of escaping parental control and trying out symbolically things that she has been warned to avoid. In addition, now is the time for acting out fantasies, fears, and strange or scary experiences, which Piaget believed helps the child diminish terror. A common occurrence around this age is for a child to play dead—if she has seen a dead bird, for example, or experienced the death of a pet. You may find her lying still and stiff, trying to see "what it feels like." Through make-believe experience she comes to alleviate her fear.

As your child approaches four you may find her going through some of the turmoil you saw at the end of two. She may be as rebellious as she once was calm, as strong-willed as she seemed compliant. The tower of blocks she once built confidently now comes crashing down as she unsteadily, but stubbornly, tries to make it bigger, higher, better. She is stretching, and as she stretches, you see the signs. Perhaps she stutters a bit, chews on clothes, seems to need extra security. It's just that she has so many new emotions and experiences that she has difficulty managing. She will learn these too. Your main job is, in fact, to see that she has as rich and rewarding an environment as possible so that she can encounter new experiences that will lead to emotional as well as motor development. You needn't push. Just talk with her, play with her, read to her, listen to her, and answer her questions. Provide her with love and a sense of security as well, and she will conquer each new stage of development when she is ready.

The Adventures of Paddy Pork by John S. Goodall. Harcourt Brace Jovanovich, 1968. $5.95. Paddy's adventures begin when he sets out to the store with his mother but spies a circus and, bitten by curiosity, steals away, out the door, away from his mother's side. A wordless book with many details to delight over, it has a clever half-page design that allows cause-and-effect scenes to be explored over and over. Also, *The Midnight Adventures of Paddy Pork* and *The Ballooning Adventures of Paddy Pork.*

A Bag Full of Pups by Dick Gackenbach. Clarion, 1981. $9.95 hardcover, $3.95 paperback. A sweet story, sprightly illustrated by Gackenbach, this tells about a man with a bag full of pups to sell and the little boy who only wants one to love.

Bedtime for Frances by Russell Hoban, illustrated by Garth Williams. Harper & Row, 1960. $9.89 hardcover, $2.95 paperback. The big hand of the clock is at twelve, the little hand is at seven—that means it's time for bed. But first Frances needs her teddy bear, doll, kisses, and a rhyming alphabet, because she's afraid of tigers or monsters or spiders. This manages to treat the subject of children's nighttime fears in an endearing but realistic way. Written by the author of the adult novel *Riddley Walker*.

Benny Bakes a Cake by Eve Rice. Greenwillow, 1981. $11.25. A story for birthday kids or for any preschoolers who know what it's like when you try to help out at home. Kids who can't seem to do things right will like Ralph the dog, who just can't help digging into the fresh-baked cake.

Billions of Bugs by Haris Petie. Prentice-Hall, 1975. $5.95. Counting bugs in a garden is a good lesson in natural science, but that's not all—it's a rhyme and a counting lesson, all on a grandiose scale that three-year-olds will love.

Blueberries for Sal by Robert McCloskey. Viking Kestrel, 1948. $8.95. *Kerplink, kerplank, kerplunk!* Little Sal drops her blueberries into her bucket but eats them up just as fast. In this classic story Sal and her mother, out blueberry picking, get all mixed up with Little Bear and his mother on Blueberry Hill.

A Boy, a Dog, and a Frog by Mercer Mayer. Dial, 1967. $3.50. A wonderful wordless gem about a boy and a dog who set off to catch a frog, and the mishaps that occur. When they finally give up, the frog is so sad that he comes running after them. The humorous incongruity of a frog leaping after boy and dog and arriving at their house will tickle three-year-olds' fancies.

Building a House by Byron Barton. Greenwillow, 1981. $10.25 hardcover, $3.95 Picture Puffin paperback. In colorful but very simple pictures, the author/illustrator shows the steps that go into making a house. This is the kind of book that is so well targeted to a very young child's ability to understand and conceptualize progression that its value is not just for kids who want to know how a house is built—it's for any child (in fact, most children) who likes to find out the hows and whys of any topic.

Caps for Sale by Esphyr Slobodkina. Addison Wesley, 1940. $7.95 hardcover, $2.25 Scholastic paperback. In the very funny old folktale a peddler carries his wares on top of his head—checked, gray, brown, blue, and red caps. But monkeys soon intervene to bring delightful confusion to his careful arrangment. The sight of the peddler with his tower of caps on his head as he goes to sleep and the next picture of him waking up to find them gone are a marvelous surprise. Children for generations have giggled with glee to see the mischievous monkeys galore sport the caps as the peddler's anger mounts. Finally the relentless monkeys throw them down on the ground, and order reigns again.

Cat Count by Betsy Lewin. Dodd, Mead, 1981. $5.95. "I have one cat, a fat cat, a fun cat. I have one cat . . . my sister has two." That's how this simple, lively counting book of cats starts off, and it rollicks its way up to sixty. We see cats that belong to various other relatives, a teacher, a preacher, and so on. Cat howlers, jivers, fiddlers, cats proper and divine. Count them all up at the end, and just see how the number skyrockets when kittens come.

Changes, Changes by Pat Hutchins. Macmillan, 1971. $10.95. The author/illustrator shows without words how blocks become *other* things: a house afire, a fire truck, a boat afloat. For young block-building tykes who've developed a capacity for symbolic play, not just structure-building, this colorful picture book brings the experience to paper.

Chicken Soup with Rice: A Book of Months by Maurice Sendak. Harper & Row, 1962. $9.89. The months are listed in verse that speaks of wonderful fun in different seasons, and best of all, every month is a month for chicken soup with rice. This is also one of four Sendak books included in the tiny, beguiling boxed set called *The Nutshell Library*. The others are *Alligators All Around: An Alphabet; One Was Johnny: A Counting Book;* and *Pierre: A Cautionary Tale.* (Boxed set: $8.95, with all books in the mini-size of 2⅞ inches by 3⁷⁄₁₆ inches.)

Circles, Triangles and Squares by Tana Hoban. Macmillan, 1974. $10.95. Three-year-olds' conceptual growth and love for details should be immensely gratified by Hoban's photographs that show objects with these shapes. Others well recommended for this year are *Count and See* and *Look Again!,* both of which will afford the three- to four-year-old many hours of enjoyment, identifying all there is to be seen in Hoban's photos. *Count and See* (1972, $10.95 hardcover, $2.25 paperback) gives the numeral on the left corresponding to a right-hand page that is a photograph of objects for kids to count.

Come Away from the Water, Shirley by John Burningham. Harper & Row, 1977. $9.89 hardcover, $3.95 paperback. Parents sitting in lounge-chairs admonish Shirley with all sorts of mundane cautions she should heed at the beach. But they're obviously not looking at what Shirley's into: She's out on the sea with a ship of pirates. The droll humor of the situation, not to mention the outright fun of Shirley's wild antics, make this a winner.

Corduroy by Don Freeman. Viking Kestrel, 1968. $8.95 hardcover, $3.50 paperback. A bear who once lived in the toy department of a big store, Corduroy ventures out from his small domain into the store when he goes in search of a lost button. But he's back in place when a girl named Lisa spies him and at last gives him a real home. Lots of love and affection are exuded by this story, and the fantasy of toys coming to life in the department store is sure to delight three-year-olds. Also, *A Pocket for Corduroy*.

The Country Bunny and the Little Gold Shoes by DuBose Heyward, pictures by Marjorie Flack. Houghton Mifflin, 1939, 1967. $9.95 hardcover, $3.50 paperback. A moving and lovely story, this is on the longish side compared with some newer stories, but it's not to be missed for reading aloud at Eastertime, springtime, or anytime. Mother Cottontail had always wanted to be one of the five Easter bunnies, but being a country bunny, she grew up to raise a family of twenty-one little rabbits instead. But when they are able to take care of themselves and the house, and a fifth Easter bunny is sought, who gets the opportunity? Cottontail, because she is swift and wise and kind. She is given a difficult assignment, but with the gift of a pair of special gold shoes, Cottontail completes her mission. A tribute to a mother's often unheralded qualities.

Curious George by H. A. Rey. Houghton Mifflin, 1941. $8.95 hardcover, $2.95 paperback. One youngster once wrote the author and asked, "Why does Curious George always have to be so *curious*?" Perhaps Rey had a three-year-old in mind when dreaming up George, the small monkey whose curious nature leads him into adventure. Three-year-olds will not only identify and establish a lifelong bond with the endearing monkey—they'll likely want to follow his lead! Other Curious George books to note are *Curious George Takes a Job, Curious George Gets a Medal,* and *Curious George Learns the Alphabet*. George also stars in a book to help small children overcome their fears of a hospital visit, *Curious George Goes to the Hospital*. It's a delight as well as an aid.

Farm Alphabet Book by Jane Miller. Prentice-Hall, 1983. $7.95. From A to Z, photos and text show, with beautiful accuracy, fruits and animals and foods and machinery found on a farm. A wonderful introduction to farm life, besides being an instructive alphabet book. Its companion, *Farm Counting Book,* first takes the reader from one to ten, then has pages of pictures that are captioned with questions such as "How many cats are there?" "Is there a bowl of milk for each cat?" Get involved in this book, see what is part of life on the

Farm
Alphabet Book

Jane Miller

farm along with your child, and witness his excitement at counting up what he has learned to identify.

Follow the River by Lydia Dabcovich. Dutton, 1980. $8.95. The cycle of a river from high up in the mountains, where it starts as a little stream, to where it flows finally into the city and out to sea is the story in this book. Good for teaching natural science as well as for the enjoyment of the details of the colored woodcut scenes. Should help children conceptualize about what happens to things as they move from place to place—they remain; they don't vanish.

Fuzzy Rabbit by Rosemary Billam, illustrated by Vanessa Julian-Ottie. Random House, 1984. $1.50 Pictureback® paperback. A sweet story that revolves around the theme of a favorite toy's feeling of rejection after being set aside for a new doll. But Fuzzy Rabbit needn't despair—the worn, old faithful friend to Ellen eventually gets his due: Ellen puts on her nurse's cap and stitches him up like new.

George and Martha by James Marshall. Houghton Mifflin, 1972. $7.95 hardcover, $2.25 paperback. As three-year-olds become interested in other children and capable of handling cooperative behavior, they become engrossed in friendship. What better story of the ups and downs of a friendship to start them off on than Marshall's hippo tales? George and Martha's friendship survives misunderstandings, petty jealousy, bossiness, and vanity through graceful humor in the face of crises. Also, *George and Martha Rise and Shine, George and Martha Back in Town,* and *George and Martha Tons of Fun,* all follow-up stories that follow the same format as the original.

Georgie by Robert Bright. Doubleday, 1959. $7.95 hardcover, $2.50 paperback. Georgie is a friendly little ghost who pleasantly haunts the Whitaker family's house. In this and the numerous other titles in which he stars, Georgie's most memorable attribute is the kindness of the deeds he performs. Also, *Georgie to the Rescue, Georgie Goes West,* and *Georgie and the Robbers.*

Good Night, Fred by Rosemary Wells. Dial, 1981. $8.50. I love this book because it so wonderfully depicts a child's misconception about what happens when Grandma calls: He thinks she is *in* the phone. Add to that a great deal of sibling warmth amid the frustrations of babysitting, and a secondary fear-of-bedtime theme, and this comes out to be a splendid read-aloud for kids who are not too old to empathize with Fred's misconceptions but just old enough to feel they've conquered them.

Growing Up Series by Derek Hall, illustrated by John Butler. Pantheon, 1984. **Otter Swims, Panda Climbs,** and **Tiger Runs**. $4.95 each. Laminated board covers give merely an inkling of what's inside these handsome picture books, and although these small, slim volumes are not inexpensive, they present factual information told as a story that toddlers will love to listen to, and also subtly colored, beautiful illustrations that are ideal for discussion. Baby otter learning

to swim will evoke empathy from your young listener, who will take in natural science at the same time. The baby animals' growing-up experiences are adorable but decidedly *not* fluff.

Harold and the Purple Crayon by Crockett Johnson. Harper & Row, 1955. $8.89 hardcover, $1.95 paperback. Harold decides to go for a walk in the moonlight, so he takes his purple crayon along and draws the moon, then a path to walk on, then a forest to walk into. With the purple crayon always ready, he gets into and out of adventure and ends up safe in bed at last. This 1950s classic was a wordless book that stayed so vividly in my mind that when I took it out to look at twenty-three years later, I couldn't believe it wasn't in full-color (the drawings use only purple and black). Yet it stirred up such imagination that after only a couple of rereadings, I knew why it had always seemed to be in full color: It went straight for my imagination, where all my childhood fantasies had taken place in living color. A book not to be missed. Also, *Harold's ABC*, *Harold's Circus*, and *Harold's Trip to the Sky*.

Hello Kitty's Paper Kiss by Sarah Bright, illustrated by Bruce McCowin. Random House, 1982. $3.50. Hello Kitty, that two-dimensional little girl cat, feels sad when Daddy goes away, but a kiss from him on the phone and a kiss in a letter help Kitty feel better. A simple book that helps small children feel better about a situation that can make them anxious or unhappy.

Here a Chick, There a Chick by Bruce McMillan. Lothrop, Lee & Shepard, 1983. $11.00. Photos of a most golden chick illustrate concepts like here and there, up and down, stand and sit. McMillan's viewpoint shines through, and what he sees—and what we see—are humor and joy, not just the lesson of the concepts. This book is as good as a visit to a farm.

A Hole Is to Dig by Ruth Krauss, pictures by Maurice Sendak. Harper & Row, 1952. $3.95. A first book of "definitions," one might say, but it's really a whole lot more. Filled with relative definitions like "Toes are to dance on," the book is brimming with wonderful childlike quotable remembrances—"Snow is to roll in," "Arms are to hug with." Help your child pour forth with more!

Little Red Cap by the Brothers Grimm, illustrated by Lisbeth Zwerger. William Morrow, 1983. $9.95. The Austrian artist has inspired this story with her magic. Her style has been described as being in the tradition of Arthur Rackham, but you don't have to know who Rackham was to love Zwerger. She uses ink and wash to create a special aura for the classic Grimms' tale of the little red-hooded girl who encounters a wolf on the way to her grandmother's house.

Martin's Hats by Joan W. Blos, illustrated by Marc Simont. William Morrow, 1984. $9.50. Simont's drawings bring to life the fantasies of Martin, a small boy with many hats and many adventures—one for each hat—that take him from exploring to firefighting to train engineering and land him back in bed, nightcap on, asleep.

Mary Alice, Operator Number 9 by Jeffrey Allen, illustrated by James Marshall. Little, Brown, 1976. $7.95 hardcover, $2.95 Puffin Books paperback. Mary Alice is the "time" operator and is indispensable—she never makes mistakes! Then she gets sick—and worries how the job will get done without her. Children will laugh to see how inept everyone is at Mary Alice's job—including Boss Chicken himself! A lovely story that manages to be warm and funny at the same time.

Mike Mulligan and His Steam Shovel by Virginia Lee Burton. Houghton Mifflin, 1939, 1967. $9.95 hardcover, $3.50 paperback. The story of the red steam shovel named Mary Anne and loyal Mike Mulligan the operator is familiar to generations. Burton's mastery of anthropomorphism is at its height here, and kids become totally involved in Mary Anne and Mike Mulligan's successful attempt to prove they are needed and not obsolete in Popperville. Read this and hear your child cheer them on as they dig the cellar of the town hall.

Millions of Cats by Wanda Gág. Coward, McCann, 1928, 1956. $7.95 hardcover, $2.95 paperback. A peasant goes in search of a cat to keep himself and his wife company, and he returns with "hundreds of cats, thousands of cats, millions and billions and trillions of cats"! A hit with three-year-old silliness, just perfect for repeating over and over and over—and an easy-to-listen-to, easy-to-read recommendation for group story hours as well as individual sittings.

Mr. Brown Can Moo! Can You? Dr. Seuss's Book of Wonderful Noises. Random House, 1970. $4.95. A goldfish's kiss? That's only one example of the delightfully absurd sound effects called forth here, with the noise printed in big colorful letters.

The Mitten by Alvin Tresselt, illustrated by Yaroslava Mills. Lothrop, Lee & Shepard, 1964. $10.80 hardcover. Scholastic paperback, 1984. $2.50. A lost mitten becomes home to many animals of the wood, stretching until it can finally stretch no more. A classic fantasy, this is illustrated simply but with plenty of action depicted.

My First Book of Nature: The Duck, The Frog, The Fox, and **The Butterfly** by Angela Sheehan, illustrated by Maurice Pledger and Bernard Robinson. Simon & Schuster, 1983. $1.98 each. Wonderful science books for reading aloud, these tell stories, not just facts, yet they are completely informational, not fiction. We learn of the life cycles of each of these creatures and have the pleasure of experiencing some of the lushest, most beautiful illustrations done for children's books in any genre.

My Nursery School by Harlow Rockwell. Greenwillow, 1976. $10.95. For first-time preschoolers this is an inspiring book. A first-person narrator simply describes all the activities, people, and things that happen at nursery school in one day.

My Red Umbrella by Robert Bright. William Morrow, 1959. $3.95 paperback. Simple vocabulary and merry drawings make this a delight. The little red umbrella becomes a shelter for a menagerie of animals, all escaping from the rain, and keeps being big enough no matter how many come for shelter.

My World series by Anne and Harlow Rockwell. Macmillan, 1981–1984. $7.95 to $8.95 each. *My Back Yard* shows the fun a little girl has at play, while *When I Go Visiting* has a boy describing his overnight visit to his grandparents' apartment. The stories are all told in short first-person narrative, while realistically depicted in soft colors. What makes them useful is that they take into account small children's feelings of accomplishment over events or surroundings, first attempts at independence, and self-pride. The books will give you insight into the importance three-year-olds place on what can seem like minor, everyday happenings—and the books reinforce the toddler's right to feel good about handling such occurrences. Others in the series include *Sick in Bed, I Play in My Room, Can I Help?, Happy Birthday to Me, How My Garden Grew,* and *I Love My Pets.*

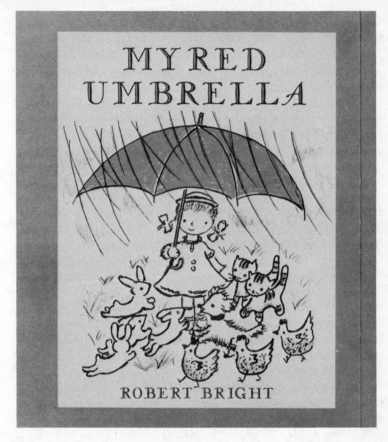

Nobody Asked Me If I Wanted a Baby Sister by Martha Alexander. Dial, 1971. $7.95. Oliver puts Bonnie in his wagon and tries to peddle her to another family, but when it seems as if she wants only to be with him, he changes his mind about his baby sister.

"Oh No, Cat!" by Janice May Udry, illustrated by Mary Chalmers. Macmillan, 1976. $5.95. A ''sweet'' cat is actually clumsily mischievous, causing Dad's outrage, but the rest of the family is on Cat's side. Mischievous preschoolers will identify with Cat, as will cat fanciers and any reader who's ever had to deal with a new-pet adjustment.

One Monday Morning by Uri Shulevitz. Scribner's, 1967. $11.95 hardcover, $3.95 paperback. The droll humor of this tale is remarkable. What happens is one Monday morning the King, the Queen, and the Prince came to visit. "But I wasn't home," the narrator tells us matter-of-factly. So, adding a new person to the royal entourage each day, the King *et al.* return, trudging up the boy's apartment house stairs and being turned away, because he's never home—until Sunday, when he is. Facing-page art shows the mundane places the boy is while missing his regal visitors. And at the end he's left alone with a deck of cards, in a poignant but hope-filled scene. The power of the imagination to create happiness is spoken for here.

On Market Street by Arnold Lobel and Anita Lobel. Greenwillow, 1981. $8.95. A Caldecott Honor Book. What to buy on Market Street? Three-year-olds will get a chance to exercise their penchant for pointing out the details aplenty in this alphabetical display of wares, decoratively designed by Anita Lobel.

Play with Me by Marie Hall Ets. Viking Kestrel, 1955. $12.95 hardcover, $3.95 paperback. A small child wants to play with her meadow friends, but she scares them away with her overtures until she at last learns she must let them alone so they can grow accustomed to her. Then they will have trust and come to her. Presenting a valuable lesson in patience, this softly told book illuminates what we sometimes mistakenly term the "modern" sensibility of needing space. This gives the child a wonderful reason for respecting privacy, as seen in the animal world. Also by the author, *Just Me* and *In the Forest*, available in Picture Puffin paperbacks for $3.50 each.

Round Trip by Ann Jonas. Greenwillow, 1983. $8.50. A black-and-white graphic rendering of a trip "from our neighborhood" to the city and back again, the ingeniously designed artwork is to be looked at both right side up for the trip there and upside down for the trip home. This is like getting two books in one, with a fun story besides.

The Snowy Day by Ezra Jack Keats. Viking Kestrel, 1962. $10.95 hardcover, $3.50 paperback. In this simple story about a small boy's experience with snow, he makes tracks in it, watches it melt, revels in it. Who couldn't have fun along with him?

The Story of Ferdinand by Munro Leaf, drawings by Robert Lawson. Viking Kestrel, 1936. $9.95. The bull who likes to sit and smell the flowers gets wrongly drafted to fight the matador in the ring. No one can keep Ferdinand's true peaceful nature a secret for long, though, and the uproar he causes when he refuses to fight is a scene that all children will relish.

Strega Nona by Tomie dePaola. Prentice-Hall, 1975. $11.95 hardcover, $5.95 paperback. A Caldecott Honor Book. Mellow color but a lively story show Big Anthony, who tries to make Strega Nona's magic pasta pot work its magic for him and then can't stop it. Soon the whole house is hilariously filled with pasta, and only Strega Nona can save the day. Three-year-olds entering into the silly stage should adore this predicament, and will laugh to see Big Anthony literally have to eat his way out of the fix.

Swimmy by Leo Lionni. Pantheon, 1969. $7.00. The story of one little fish who escaped being swallowed and marshaled all the other little fish together to act as one against the big fish will give three-year-olds a nice feeling of power in the face of larger presences. How Swimmy overcomes his particular size problem is warm and wonderful.

Tikki Tikki Tembo, retold by Arlene Mosel, illustrated by Blair Lent. Holt, Rinehart & Winston, 1968. $9.95 hardcover. Scholastic paperback, 1984. $2.50. Tikki Tikki Tembo-no sa rembo-chari bari ruchi-pip peri pembo is the name of the eldest Chinese son, while the second son is named merely Chang. Then Tikki Tikki Tembo falls into the well, and Chang must first tell his mother and then tell the Old Man with the ladder. Hurry, Chang! Readers will wait in suspense but giggle with hilarity at the predicament of a boy who gets out of breath trying to say his brother's ridiculously long name when the brother's life is endangered.

Too Much Noise by Ann McGovern, illustrated by Simms Taback. Houghton Mifflin, 1967. $10.95. Peter has a house full of noise—and each query to the wise man seems only to add more: a cow (that says Moo Moo), a donkey (Hee Haw), a sheep (Baa Baa), and so on. One by one he lets them go just as he acquired them, and at last his own house noises seem nice and quiet. Noises make this a fun read-aloud, but be prepared for plenty of shouting along!

Trucks by Art Seiden. Platt & Munk, 1983. $3.50. A catalogue, good-sized, with its board pages picturing all kinds of trucks, from fire truck to concrete mixer to tow truck. For truck enthusiasts and small vehicle-lovers.

The Velveteen Rabbit by Margery Williams, illustrated by William Nicholson. Doubleday, 1926, 1958. $7.95 hardcover, $2.25 Avon/Camelot paperback. This is the story of the toy who stuck by the Boy even through illness, until at last the Velveteen Rabbit is visited by the nursery magic fairy, who turns him into Real and gives him a home with other rabbits. Touching and tender, and as memorable as any child's own favorite stuffed animal. I recommend the original edition, with Nicholson's hauntingly rendered illustrations.

William's Doll by Charlotte Zolotow, pictures by William Pene du Bois. Harper & Row, 1972. $6.89. The plight of a boy who wants a doll ''to hug and to cradle and to take to the park'' is explored here in a tenderly realistic way.

Chapter Seven

FROM FOUR TO FIVE YEARS

*F*our-year-olds are some of the most boisterous, exuberant children of all. They seem constantly filled with the desire to be doing something active, moving quickly from one activity to the next—hardly the same children who repeated an activity over and over until they got it right.

A four-year-old doesn't have to spend as much time experimenting but can do a thing once and master it. This age has been termed expansive by child-development specialists, and it's easy to see why. Your child's emotions may seem to you to run wild. She may even shock you with the bad language she may use as easily as she uses nonsense talk, silly words, or sounds; it's as if words can't always adequately express what she feels. That may seem ironic to parents who see the other side of their four-year-old as so much more mature than she was at two or three.

The four-year-old also has the capability of being quite a bit more articulate, since her language skills have developed considerably. And as much as she may appear to be out of control at times, not only does the four-year-old want and like to have rules and limits set, but you can begin to trust her and consider her ready to act responsibly in certain situations. In *The Early Childhood Years* (Perigee, 1983), the Caplans stress, however, that because children of this age can seem capable of being so mature, parents may tend to overestimate their child's ability to bear demands. Don't burden her with too many dos and don'ts, and remember that no matter how old your four-year-old may seem, she is still young and struggling to learn.

Your four-year-old is also developing her fine motor skills—she has enough control to be able to use blunt scissors, cut along a line, copy letter forms, and thread beads—showing an enormous new growth in powers of concentration as well as attention to detail. In addition to boisterous outdoor play, she loves clay modeling, drawing, jigsaw puzzles, finger painting, and puppet shows. Now is the time when an old sock or a brown paper bag can become a hand puppet, with your child exhibiting amazing dramatic capabilities.

Now is the age when your child begins to learn a sense of time as clock time. She can count to thirty, knows the seasons, and is beginning to understand the relationship between seasons and activities. And she is ever curious. She asks why, when, and how questions constantly.

Four-year-olds love language. Parents begin to hear fantastic stories that often make them wonder where their child got *that* idea from. Your child may be exercising her imagination, she may be stringing together bits and pieces of things into one story, or she may be combining reality and fantasy as she tacks make-believe details onto actual events. But just because children of this age seem capable of making up their own stories doesn't mean you should cease feeding their imaginations. This imaginative storytelling interest only shows how much all the reading and talking to your child have actually meant! Keep her mind freshly fed with new and wonderful tales to ponder over, to learn from, and from which to find characters to grow to love. The nursery rhymes you read to a baby to lull her to sleep are now to be freshly explored for their nonsense words, strange situations, silly language, and rhymes.

Stories about you as a child, your child as a baby, and people being good or bad reflect his interest in the past, his self-interest, and his interest in rules and boundaries. And remember that, despite the wild imagination your four-year-old may be exhibiting, you will see an extreme concreteness in his thinking now as well. He is quite observant in matters that concern him. As he grows more social, attends preschool, and becomes more accustomed to playing with other children, he will grow to develop strong likes and dislikes for people he sees frequently, but you will also note that these strong likes and dislikes change frequently. In fact, the four-year-old has a tremendous interest in joining in group activity, and may even begin to organize groups without the prompting or aid of an adult. As four-year-olds near five, you will also notice the emergence of group positions—leaders and followers. And they are always proud of their parents and may often try to tell strangers all about you!

Subjects of particular interest to four-year-olds are varied. For example, one prevalent interest of four-year-olds seems to be fire, and all of its associations—they love firemen, fire trucks, stories about firehouses, and facts about how fires are fought. Feed this interest positively; many writers and illustrators have approached the topic from all sorts of angles. Four-year-olds may have other interests you will view as absurd. Silly poems and stories now vie equally with the familiar for popularity with four-year-olds. And they may enjoy switching back and forth, making the familiar silly, or finishing a nonsense tale off with something right out of the ordinary. Your child may insist on keeping one or two important factual details in a nonsense or make-believe game. The paradox is obvious—just as he loves adventure, for himself and in stories, he loves to have rules for himself and to hear about rules for others. He loves to hear exaggeration, but he loves to be praised honestly for his accomplishments. Follow your child's lead—join in with his silly games, but when he is not in the mood, don't assume he will want to participate if you introduce some silliness. You might find him totally recalcitrant!

Animals in the Wild: Tiger, Elephant, Monkey, and Panda. Random House, 1984. $1.50 each, paperback. Like small paperbound documentaries, these are filled with photos and tell the story of each of these handsome wild beasts. For nature lovers, especially, the photos will depict the real qualities of animals often seen fictionalized or fantasized in picture books, so they give a balance to those imagined characteristics that fictional literature often gives the animals. That is not to say, though, that these small books are not every bit as imaginative as fiction picture books—in fact, the stories they tell, because true, have a different and wonderful kind of power to them.

The Big Snow by Berta and Elmer Hader. Macmillan, 1949. $8.95. A Caldecott Medal Winner. A lovely book that shows how winter comes to the woodland animals—Mrs. Cottontail and her rabbits, Mrs. Chipmunk—and how the people in the stone house help out when the big snow makes it difficult for the animals to find food.

The Book of Pigericks by Arnold Lobel. Harper & Row, 1983. $9.89. If you're wondering what pigericks are, why, they're original limericks about pigs, of course. Old pigs, young pigs, sweet and nasty, poor and rich, rude or pleasant, they're all represented here, and they're suspiciously close to humans in nature. Lobel's art is vibrantly colored and detailed, a match for the wit of his verse.

The Cat in the Hat by Dr. Seuss. Random House, 1956. $4.95. Why Dr. Seuss is a perennial favorite could be the subject of a book in itself. The simplest reason is that his words sound wonderful to children's ears. Kids who are old enough to appreciate the silly antics of the story have a second reason for loving Seuss, and when your child begins to read by herself, she will love the feeling of accomplishment she gets from these books, because they are just perfect for beginning readers too. Also by Dr. Seuss: *The Cat in the Hat Comes Back, And to Think That I Saw It on Mulberry Street, Green Eggs and Ham*, and *How the Grinch Stole Christmas.*

A Chair for My Mother by Vera B. Williams. Greenwillow, 1982. $10.25. So much to pore over here, but the warm story comes first. The narrator tells of her family's plan to buy her mother a chair: All savings go into a big glass jar. Will it ever fill up? Some tense moments come when a fire ruins the family's apartment, but at last the jar is filled, and they pick out the chair they want. Williams's bright paintings say so much about this all-female family's tight-knit outlook, the young narrator's determination, and the joy that shines through in spite of some setbacks. Watch the borders around the paintings change on each spread, as do small details on every right-hand page.

Cloudy with a Chance of Meatballs by Judi Barret, illustrated by Ron Barret. Atheneum, 1978. $11.95. You might like to try this story with preschoolers who are particularly fond of hyperbole. Here Grandpa tells the kids a story about a town where no one ever had to go to the market—food came like the weather, and it hailed hot dogs, rained hamburgers, and so on. What does the town do, though, when the weather takes a turn for the worse? They abandon their village and sail to safety on white-bread sailboats!

Crictor by Tomi Ungerer. Harper & Row, 1958. $9.89 hardcover, $3.25 paperback. Crictor the boa constrictor is a most accommodating pet, and that characteristic is sure to prove delightful to any child you should read this to. So helpful a pet is Crictor that he learns to play with little boys and girls, fashions the letters of the alphabet in Madame Bodot's class, and so on until eventually Crictor even stops a burglar. Truly Crictor is a hero for all, and well deserving of the park named in his honor.

The Do-Something Day by Joe Lasker. Viking Kestrel, 1982. $12.95 hardcover, $1.95 paperback. On a cheery day everyone is too busy for Bernie, so he decides to run away. What the reader gains are the benefits of the neighborhood tour he takes to inform everyone of his plan! As Bernie tells his neighborhood friends that no one needs him, he finds they all do, even his parents, who need him to love. It's not sappy—it's just right, because the art is bright and cheery and forthright.

The Duchess Bakes a Cake by Virginia Kahl. Scribner's, 1955. $7.95 hardcover, $2.95 paperback. Rollicking rhyme and drawings in red, green, and black help this story swing along. Hilarity ensues when the duchess decides to bake a "light luscious delectable cake," and it rises and rises and rises and takes her along with it. Only her smallest daughter seems able to bring her down, when her hunger prompts her to want to eat some of the cake, and the rest of the family and court follow suit.

The Easter-Egg Artists by Adrienne Adams. Scribner's, 1976. $12.95. As Orson decides what kind of artist he wants to be, the Abbott rabbits tool around, undertaking various artistic enterprises. Great fun for little businesspeople, it will hit just perfectly those who've already begun thinking about what they want to be when they grow up. Rabbit-loving little kids won't be able to resist, either.

Feelings by Aliki. Greenwillow, 1984. $10.25. All the common human feelings that we experience are wonderfully shown here in small scenarios—pride, anger, guilt, loneliness, happiness, and love are portrayed through the common events kids identify with. Aliki's nearly miniature-size line art does much to alleviate any of the difficult-to-handle "heaviness" that you might be afraid to find in such a book. She is a master of bringing a lighthearted tone to deeply felt topics, and here the two balance each other. This book should stimulate much parent-and-child or teacher-and-child discussion. If you talk about each feeling with your child, tell him you've felt that way and give him the opportunity to share his happy and sad, good and bad, feelings too.

Fire! Fire! by Gail Gibbons. T. Y. Crowell, 1984. $9.89. For four-year-olds with an intense interest in the subject, here's an informational book about the topic. It not only explores different types of fires but also shows different places fires start, how they are fought, and by whom. Both colorful and informative, the book provides the kind of details that will make it a much used resource book as well as a fun book.

Firehouse by Peter Spier. Doubleday, 1981. $3.95. A Peter Spier Village Book. Shaped like a firehouse, this has all the excitement of the story it tells about a fire and how the firehouse moves into action. And it contains a mini picture catalogue of equipment, a must for young firefighters-to-be.

The Five Chinese Brothers by Kurt Wiese and Claire Huchet Bishop. Coward, McCann, 1938. $7.95. Try this with children who think cartoons and comic books are the only places to find superheroes! Each of these five brothers has an amazing power that he uses to pull a trick on the executioner trying to mete out punishment to the first brother, who drowned a greedy boy. Four-year-olds will be enthralled with the brothers' superpowers and delighted with the switches they pull.

The Giving Tree by Shel Silverstein. Harper & Row, 1964. $8.89. "Once there was a tree . . . and she loved a little boy." This now classic story about the unlimited capacity of some to love is shown through the allegory of the tree who gives and gives and needs only the little boy's need for her to make her happy. And as he grows older and she gives all, her love still is not depleted, until finally, even as a mere stump who can offer him a resting place, she is still happy.

Hide-and-Seek Fog by Alvin Tresselt, illustrated by Roger Duvoisin. Lothrop, Lee & Shepard, 1965. $9.84. As the fog comes in over Cape Cod, we can practically feel it enshroud us, through both the muted, milky shading of the art and the imagery used in the text. This wonderful read-aloud explores more than just fog as a natural phenomenon, or how fog changes the appearance of an everyday world into a strange, half-frightening, half-magical place. It also shows how it affects the lives of the people as it grinds all normal living to a halt.

Hooray for Me by Remy Charlip and Lillian Moore, pictures by Vera B. Williams. Four Winds Press, 1975. $8.95. A celebration of the individuality that makes us all unique and one that four-year-olds and older kids in particular will appreciate. Splashy, colorful illustrations fit perfectly these first-person descriptions: "I'm my dog's walker," "I'm my dream's dreamer," "I'm my aunt's nephew." A great answer to any child's questions about himself, and a book nearly "readable" even by pre-readers, because of the repetition of certain words.

Horton Hears a Who by Dr. Seuss. Random House, 1954. $3.95. Swinging rhyme tells a playful story about an elephant who hears the voice of a very small person called a Who (the Whos have an entire town built in a speck of dust). Horton the helpful helps them find their voices against bigger enemies, a situation any small child can easily empathize with. You'll love reading this aloud to your preschoolers, who will get involved in the plight of the Whos and in Horton's efforts on their behalf.

The House on East 88th Street by Bernard Waber. Houghton Mifflin, 1962. $10.95 hardcover, $2.95 paperback. The Primms move in to find a crocodile at home in their bathtub—Lyle, of course, and the only, most appropriate way to describe him is, indeed, as lovable. He has the charming ability to walk into readers' hearts just as he walked into the Primms'. Once you meet Lyle in this book, you'll want to reacquaint your children and yourself with him in *Lovable Lyle, Lyle and the Birthday Party,* and *Lyle, Lyle Crocodile.*

Ira Sleeps Over by Bernard Waber. Houghton Mifflin, 1972. $10.95 hardcover, $3.95 paperback. Free-flowing humor and characters gentle and cynical (Ira's sister) all get involved in Ira's decision over whether or not to take his teddy bear to a friend's house. A funny, tender story of trust and friendship that says it can be okay not to have to grow up too fast.

Jim's Dog Muffins by Miriam Cohen, illustrated by Lillian Hoban. Greenwillow, 1984. $10.00. A book that deals with death and the adjustment to death we all face. Here it is Jim's dog who has died, and Jim is so sad that not even his classmate's letter to him can seem to help. When Jim finally gives vent to his feelings, we are all moved. A cathartic experience, this can be useful for kids coping with the death of a beloved animal or someone close to the child.

Just Us Women by Jennette Caines, illustrated by Pat Cummings. Harper & Row, 1982. $9.89 hardcover, $3.95 paperback. The relationship of a niece and her aunt is only one aspect of this book that's sweet. The story is told in a relaxed and happily carefree manner. The details of some of what the niece imagines they will do on their car trip together (with no parents or passengers to tell them no) also have sweetness. It's nice to see such friendship between generations.

Katy No-Pocket by Emmy Payne, pictures by H. A. Rey. Houghton Mifflin, 1944, 1972. $8.95. A kangaroo mother doesn't have a pocket for her son, Freddy, so she ventures in search of one and finds dozens of possible pockets in the city. The solution to her problem makes more than one little animal happy.

Little Red Riding Hood by Trina Schart Hyman. Holiday House, 1983. $13.95. The author/illustrator borders the text in a quiltlike frame that echoes the larger illustration in its detail, and each frame is unique. Spellbinding colors transfix the reader—warm and lovely tones soon grow nearly frightening, conveying all the drama of the story and the mysterious nature of the forest Red Riding Hood travels in. Quite different from, and yet as good a choice as, Zwerger's version of the classic story (see page 84). Also well illustrated by Hyman is *Rapunzel*, retold by Barbara Rogansky (Holiday House, 1982. $12.95).

Little Tim and the Brave Sea Captain by Edward Ardizzone. Picture Puffin, 1977, 1982. $3.50 paperback. Lovely sea-washed illustrations for adventure-loving children, or those with a fondness for, or yearning to see, the ocean. The hero, Little Tim, is just the kind of brave and curious boy to inspire shy preschoolers or to elicit cheers from boisterous and bold youngsters.

Max by Rachel Isadora. Macmillan, 1976. $9.95. Max on his way to baseball practice kills some time in his sister's dancing class—and finds it to be a great warm-up for baseball. The joy expressed in Isadora's illustrations cannot be understated—they'll have little four-year-olds leaping with exuberance with just the slightest bit of encouragement and will give deep pleasure to the adult who reads the story.

Old Sadie and the Christmas Bear by Phyllis Reynolds Naylor, illustrated by Patricia Montgomery Newton. Atheneum, 1984. $11.95. Sadie, a nearsighted old woman, mistakes a bear for a visitor in a fur coat, and the bear, who had awakened from hibernation because of the smell of something exciting in the air, has his first Christmas. This is a warm and wonderful story of sharing, with old-fashioned Christmas details sketched into the illustrations of Sadie and her new Christmas friend Amos.

One Fine Day by Nonny Hogrogian. Macmillan, 1971. $12.95 hardcover, $2.95 paperback. A Caldecott Medal Winner. When Fox laps up a pail of milk, the old woman he stole it from promptly cuts off his tail, and thus starts off a cumulative tale of favors to be done in order for Fox to get his tail sewn back on. Hogrogian's happy pictures, in glowing colors, bring this folk story to gorgeous life.

A Picture Book of Hanukkah by David A. Adler, illustrated by Linda Heller. Holiday House, 1982. $9.95. A simple retelling— though definitely a read-aloud selection—of the eight-day holiday of Hanukkah. It includes brief explanations of the customs we continue today: lighting the menorah candles, singing about the Hanukkah miracles, and playing dreidel games. Two other picture books of Jewish holidays are *A Picture Book of Passover* and *A Picture Book of Jewish Holidays,* both also by David A. Adler and Linda Heller. All three make fascinating reading for Jewish and non-Jewish children alike.

The Piney Woods Peddler, told by George Shannon, pictures by Nancy Tafuri. Greenwillow, 1981. $7.95. Walking through the woods, encountering a barefoot woman with a brown cow, a man with a strong black mule, a rattlesnake rattling all his rattlers, and others, the Piney Woods Peddler sings his song. He's swapping his possessions to get his dear darling daughter a shiny silver dollar. Though he ends with only a dime, his dear darling daughter thinks it shines just like a silver dollar, so all the swapping and trading was wonderfully worth the outcome. A marvelous read-aloud story, with the peddler's song making a neat refrain for all to join in: "With a wing wang waddle/And a great big straddle/And a Jack-fair-faddle/It's a long way from home."

Rotten Ralph by Jack Gantos, illustrated by Nicole Rubel. Houghton Mifflin, 1976. $8.95 hardcover, $2.50 paperback. Ralph, Sarah's deliciously naughty and funny cat, gets his comeuppance but remains endearing to his mistress. Four-year-olds will love this blatantly awful cat, who is loved in spite of himself as well as because of his nature. Also, *Worse Than Rotten Ralph* (1978) and *Rotten Ralph's Rotten Christmas* (1984).

Someone Special, Just Like You, photos by Fran Ortiz. Holt, Rinehart & Winston, 1984. $11.45. With her photographs Ortiz presents a picture of handicapped children that goes beyond their disabilities and gets to their feelings. Shown enjoying music, art, and dance class, at home and at school, sad and happy, they are portrayed honestly and in a way that puts a fresh perspective on their situations, for handicapped and nonhandicapped children alike.

Squeeze a Sneeze by Bill Morrison. Houghton Mifflin, 1977. $6.95. A book of nonsense rhymes, this one encourages readers to imitate the ones included. A good parent– or teacher–child participation book, this affords plenty of fun with verse, such as "Share a pear with a hungry bear," to mimic for sound if not sense.

Stevie by John Steptoe. Harper & Row, 1984. $10.95. A black child at first resents his foster brother but then realizes he misses him. A reissue of a 1969 title, this will interest all with sibling conflicts.

Sylvester and the Magic Pebble by William Steig. Simon & Schuster, 1969, 1984. $4.95 paperback. Sylvester Duncan, a donkey, uses a magic pebble unwisely and becomes trapped inside a rock, unable to become himself again, because in order to work magic he has to be touching the pebble. Not for a long time afterward (at least a year, and it seems like forever), it is through his parents' unwitting intervention that Sylvester becomes himself again, to the joy of all. And the satisfying conclusion is: Who could wish for more than love and family?

Tell Me a Mitzi by Lore Segal, pictures by Harriet Pincus. Farrar, Straus & Giroux, 1970. $12.95. These three stories about "Mitzi" use an interesting device—they're told to Martha by her parents when she pesters them for a Mitzi story despite however busy they are. One strongly suspects Martha is Mitzi. The fun is not only in reading about what happens to Mitzi in "Mitzi Takes a Taxi," "Mitzi Sneezes," and "Mitzi and the President" but in deciding which are real and which only might have happened—or are they all just acts of imagi-

nation? The book is, and that's the pleasure above all. If you enjoy this, you'll want to try *Tell Me a Trudy* ($10.95), illustrated by Rosemary Wells.

Tell Me Grandma, Tell Me Grandpa by Shirlee Newman, illustrated by Joan Drescher. Houghton Mifflin, 1979. $6.95. A little girl's imagination takes over when her grandparents describe her parents as children. It's fun for youngsters to think about their parents as kids, and this handles the notion merrily. Four-year-olds will likely become involved in all the funny mental pictures this conjures up and go on to imagine some of their own.

The Tenth Good Thing About Barney by Judith Viorst, illustrated by Erik Blegvad. Atheneum, 1971. $10.95. Barney was a cat whom the narrator mourns in this deeply felt and honest book. The narrator tries to get used to the idea that Barney is gone by thinking of ten good things about him, and he is at a loss for the tenth, until Barney's burial takes place and he finds out that after life, Barney will be helping the trees and flowers grow, "a pretty good job for a cat."

This Is Betsy by Gunilla Wolde. Random House, 1975. $4.99 hardcover, $1.95 paperback. Who is Betsy? A girl of many moods and games, and one who definitely doesn't believe she always has to do what is expected of her. She's just the kind of preschooler your child will identify with. Betsy tests all the limits in a humorous way.

Tight Times by Barbara Shook Hazen, pictures by Trina Schart Hyman. Viking Kestrel, 1979. $9.95 hardcover, $3.50 paperback. A book about yearnings and longings, and how a child sees reality. A small child wants a dog, but times are bad and then Dad loses his job, and the child realizes the dream doesn't have much of a chance. Until one day—a meowing from inside a garbage can changes things around.

Tin Lizzie by Peter Spier. Doubleday, 1975. $1.95 paperback. For young automobile buffs and their parents, who will enjoy reading aloud to them some of the history of the car, this book traces that history for fifty years in detailed scenes and bits of scenes. Spier's bright washes of color bring this subject to life as well as chronicle the changes that have taken place in America since the car was first introduced. Don't miss the book's endpapers: They provide one of the most beautiful looks at all the car's parts one is likely to see illustrated for this age group.

Ty's One Man Band by Mildred Pitts Walter, illustrated by Margot Tomes. Four Winds Press, 1980. $9.95 hardcover, $3.50 Scholastic paperback. Ty meets Andro, a peglegged man who intrigues the young boy with the wonderful music he creates from a spoon beating on a cup and a plate, or a piece of tissue paper on a comb. A story filled with all the noises a four-year-old will want to hear over and over, like the sound of horses dancing.

Uproar on Hollercat Hill by Jean Marzollo, pictures by Steven Kellogg. Dial, 1980. $8.95 hardcover, $3.50 paperback. Kellogg's amusingly rendered family of high-strung cats has a day of mishaps, but at last peace is restored. Rolling rhyme and brash, wild pictures capture the confusion in a lively and appealing way.

A Very Special House by Ruth Krauss, illustrated by Maurice Sendak. Harper & Row, 1953. $10.89. Let your preschooler revel in the delights to be found inside a house where all a child's wishes are indulged and nobody ever says stop.

We Can't Sleep by James Stevenson. Greenwillow, 1982. $9.50. Louie and Mary Ann can't get to sleep. So Grandpa tells them all about how he had that same problem once as a boy, and his subsequent wild stories of exploits on that night at last send the kids off to their dreams, and what a wonderful way to go. Don't miss the cartoonist's rendering of Grandpa as a boy—complete with mustache. A neat combination of zaniness and warmth.

What's Good for a Four-Year-Old? by William Cole, illustrated by Tomi Ungerer. Holt, Rinehart & Winston, 1967. A good book like this is marvelous for four-year-olds, who will love having a book written just for them. When you're done going through it and finding out what the kids in it (Bobby and Annie and Eddie) have on *their* lists, ask your four-year-old. To be fair, Cole has given the same treat to three-, five-, and six-year-olds in books that ask the same question of those age groups. No longer in print, it is still available in libraries in both hardcover and paperback.

What's That? (1979) and **Catching** (1984) by Virginia Allen Jensen. Philomel. $12.95 each. Little Shaggy and Little Rough are the characters in these picture books, which are aimed at blind children and use raised forms and figures distinguishable by feel. However, children who've loved other "touch and feel" books may also be attracted to these, so don't rule out their interest for sighted pre-schoolers. These books are spiral-bound.

When I Was Young in the Mountains by Cynthia Rylant, illus-trated by Diane Goode. Dutton, 1982. $9.95. The details of life growing up in the mountains were inspired by memories of the author's Appalachian childhood and are illuminated by warm and affectionate paintings that truly point up the pleasure and contentment of this rural way of life. A good book for kids yearning to find out about other places, and one that will be accessible to all who long for a good story.

A Woggle of Witches by Adrienne Adams. Scribner's, 1971. $9.95 hardcover, $2.95 paperback. A ghoulishly delightful record of a witches' night out. They eat spider-web bread and are amusingly frightened by small children out in costume on Halloween. Children who like to be scared won't be disappointed, but the ending is such turnabout reassurance that there'll be no nightmares afterward.

Chapter Eight
WHERE TO GET CHILDREN'S BOOKS

*I*f you are lucky, you have a full-service children's bookstore in your community or within a short riding distance from your town. This bookstore is a gem. Its proprietor likely not only knows what he or she stocks currently but also keeps abreast of what customers' needs are. This kind of specialty children's bookseller frequently acts as a consultant to keep customers satisfied, keeping a log of frequent customers' purchases, finding out how those purchases were enjoyed by the child, and noting any dissatisfactions or particular likes of the child.

"Children change as they grow. You can't assume anything about what they'll like next, but you can make educated choices. That is the kind of help we can give to the parents who come in for books," one children's bookseller said. Another said, "If a parent comes in and says her son insists on a book about dinosaurs, and if she can tell us how old he is, or if she can tell us that he likes photographs, or big books, or some other of his reading preferences, we can choose one or two that would be the best for him from the scores of informational books, pop-ups, or stories about dinosaurs."

But more than likely, unless you live in a large city or in or nearby an academic community, this type of children's bookshop does not exist for you. Go to the general bookstore closest to you, but don't expect the bookseller, unless he or she admits to a special interest in children's books, to know all there is to know. But ask for information. If you go prepared with the title and author of the book you are looking for, this general bookseller will be able to order it for you even if the store doesn't keep it in stock. Chain bookstores, like Waldenbooks and B. Dalton's, may have many of the books for children of the youngest age but may not be able to help you find others. Don't despair if chain bookstores are your only local bookstore, because it is easy to supplement book buying with book borrowing. Yes, that's right: Don't overlook your local public library.

While libraries are only now beginning to realize how important it is that their children's services extend downward to preschoolers, they will certainly be of help to you in borrowing any hardcover picture books or collections of nursery rhymes, songs, or poetry. Libraries are also increasing their selections of paperbacks. It's nice to be able to try several books at home with your child and then buy the most favorite. It certainly increases a child's pleasure to own a favorite book—something truly his own—but there is no point in buying hundreds of books your child may or may not enjoy.

Many librarians confess that they would love to be able to do more for preschool children, but that library budgets and restricted hours prevent them from doing so. If you can, talk to the children's section librarian. Libraries do respond to the interests of their communities. If you let him or her know that you and other parents would like to see more books bought for younger children, or that you would like to see the library hold story hours for preschoolers at times convenient to you, the librarian may be able to help.

A children's librarian in suburban New York spoke about how her program for preschoolers and their parents evolved. "First we set up a story hour for preschoolers. Then we opened it up to parents with toddlers, because the demand was so great. Even so, many working parents who heard how well the story hour was received felt left out and came to talk to us about holding it on a Sunday afternoon. Now we do two, one on a weekday evening, one on Sunday afternoon. Parents come in on weekdays with the kids in pajamas. We all lie down on the floor, hear stories, look at books, the kids crawl around, and pretty soon they're ready for sleep. It's a bit more lively on Sunday afternoons, but the relaxed atmosphere and sense of community is the same.''

How to Find Out About Books

There are many resources for finding out about new books.

Read reviews in magazines and newspapers. *The New York Times Book Review* publishes weekly reviews of children's books and is available in bookstores and libraries and on newsstands. *The Horn Book* magazine publishes reviews of children's books and is available for $30.00 per year from 31 St. James Avenue, Boston, Massachusetts 02116. *The Horn Book* also publishes a newsletter for parents called *Why Children's Books?*, which is available from Amy Cohn, The Horn Book, Inc., 31 St. James Avenue, Boston, Massachusetts 02116. Write for a sample copy.

Other review publications include *Parents Magazine*, 80 New Bridge Road, Bergenfield, New Jersey 07621, which publishes frequent, although irregularly timed, book review roundups. *Family Learning*, 5615 West Cermak Road, Cicero, Illinois, also publishes review roundups, and *Redbook* magazine plans to award its first Children's Picture Book of the Year honor in 1985. *Parents' Choice*, Box 185, Waban, Massachusetts 02168, (617) 965-5913, is a quarterly review of children's media—books, television, movies, records, toys, computer software, video cassettes, and games. *Cubby's Corner*, from Trespassers William, 700 Amherst NE, Albuquerque, New Mexico 87106, is a review of children's books. Send sixty cents in stamps for a sample copy.

Mail-order outlets include Book Call, located in Connecticut, which has a toll-free number (1-800-255-2665) and promises to ship ''any book anywhere in the world.'' They have a gift catalogue, or you can simply ask for the book of your choice. Please help them by knowing title, author, or both, and they will locate it for you.

Book-Stock specializes in quality children's books. Send $2.00 for their catalogue, to 44 Tee-Ar, Dept. HB, Princeton, New Jersey 08540.

Gryphon House, Inc., handles early childhood books. The address is 3706 Otis Street, P.O. Box 275, Mt. Rainier, Maryland 20712, or use their toll-free number (1-800-638-0928).

The Junior Literary Guild, 245 Park Avenue, New York, New York 10167, is a direct-mail book club especially for children. Enroll your child in membership and choose books for her now, then let her choose for herself as she gets older.

Parents Magazine's Reading Aloud & Easy Reading Program, 685 Third Avenue, New York, New York 10017, is aimed at children from two to seven years old.

Reading Rainbow

Finally, when you turn to your television, tune in a summertime children's reading program on Public Television called *Reading Rainbow*. Hosted by LeVar Burton, the show uses live action and voice-overs with art from children's books to dramatize selected picture books each week. In addition, children give book reviews of their favorite picture books and storybooks. Here is a wonderful way to use television to encourage reading!

CALDECOTT MEDAL WINNERS

*T*he Randolph Caldecott Medal has been awarded each year since 1938, under the supervision of the Association for Library Services to Children of the American Library Association, to the illustrator of the most distinguished picture book for children published in the United States during the preceding year.

1985 *St. George and the Dragon* retold by Margaret Hodges, illustrated by Trina Schart Hyman (Little, Brown)

1984 *The Glorious Flight* by Alice and Martin Provensen (Viking Kestrel)

1983 *Shadow* by Blaise Cendrars, illustrated by Marcia Brown (Scribner's)

1982 *Jumanji* by Chris Van Allsburg (Houghton Mifflin)

1981 *Fables* by Arnold Lobel (Harper & Row)

1980 *Ox-Cart Man* by Donald Hall, illustrated by Barbara Cooney (Viking Kestrel)

1979 *The Girl Who Loved Wild Horses* by Paul Goble (Bradbury Press)

1978 *Noah's Ark* by Peter Spier (Doubleday)

1977 *Ashanti to Zulu: African Traditions* by Margaret Musgrove, illustrated by Leo and Diane Dillon (Dial)

1976 *Why Mosquitos Buzz in People's Ears* by Verna Aardema, illustrated by Leo and Diane Dillon (Dial)

1975 *Arrow to the Sun* by Gerald McDermott (Viking Kestrel)

1974 *Duffy and the Devil* by Harve Zemach, illustrated by Margot Zemach (Farrar, Straus & Giroux)

1973 *The Funny Little Woman* retold by Arlene Mosel, illustrated by Blair Lent (Dutton)

1972 *One Fine Day* by Nonny Hogrogian (Macmillan)

1971 *A Story—a Story* by Gail E. Haley (Atheneum)

1970 *Sylvester and the Magic Pebble* by William Steig (Simon & Schuster)

1969 *The Fool of the World and the Flying Ship* by Arthur Ransome, illustrated by Uri Shulevitz (Farrar, Straus & Giroux)

1968 *Drummer Hoff* by Barbara Emberly, illustrated by Ed Emberly (Prentice-Hall)

1967 *Sam, Bangs and Moonshine* by Evaline Ness (Holt, Rinehart & Winston)

1966 *Always Room for One More* by Sorche Nic Leodhas, illustrated by Nonny Hogrogian (Holt, Rinehart & Winston)

1965 *May I Bring a Friend?* by Beatrice Schenk de Regniers, illustrated by Beni Montresor (Atheneum)

1964 *Where the Wild Things Are* by Maurice Sendak (Harper & Row)

1963 *The Snowy Day* by Ezra Jack Keats (Viking Kestrel)

1962 *Once a Mouse . . .* by Marcia Brown (Scribner's)

1961 *Baboushka and the Three Kings* by Ruth Robbins, illustrated by Nicholas Sidjakov (Parnassus Press/Houghton Mifflin)

1960 *Nine Days to Christmas* by Marie Hall Ets and Aurora Labastida, illustrated by Marie Hall Ets (Viking Kestrel)

1959 *Chanticleer and the Fox* adapted from Chaucer, illustrated by Barbara Cooney (T. Y. Crowell)

1958 *Time of Wonder* by Robert McCloskey (Viking)

1957 *A Tree Is Nice* by Janice May Udry, illustrated by Marc Simont (Harper & Row)

1956 *Frog Went A-Courtin'* edited by John Langstaff, illustrated by Feodor Rojanovsky (Harcourt Brace Jovanovich)

1955 *Cinderella, or the Little Glass Slipper* by Charles Perrault, translated and illustrated by Marcia Brown (Scribner's)

1954 *Madeline's Rescue* by Ludwig Bemelmans (Viking Kestrel)

1953 *The Biggest Bear* by Lynd Ward (Houghton Mifflin)

1952 *Finders Keepers* by Will, illustrated by Nicolas (Harcourt Brace Jovanovich)

1951 *The Egg Tree* by Katherine Milhous (Scribner's)

1950 *Song of the Swallows* by Leo Politi (Scribner's)

1949 *The Big Snow* by Berta and Elmer Hader (Macmillan)

1948 *White Snow, Bright Snow* by Alvin Tresselt, illustrated by Roger Duvoisin (Lothrop, Lee & Shepard)

1947 *The Little Island* by Golden MacDonald, illustrated by Leonard Weisgard (Doubleday)

1946 *The Rooster Crows,* traditional Mother Goose, illustrated by Maud and Miska Petersham (Macmillan)

1945 *Prayer for a Child* by Rachel Field, illustrated by Elizabeth Orton Jones (Macmillan)

1944 *Many Moons* by James Thurber, illustrated by Louis Slobodkin (Harcourt Brace Jovanovich)

1943 *The Little House* by Virginia Lee Burton (Houghton Mifflin)

1942 *Make Way for Ducklings* by Robert McCloskey (Viking Kestrel)

1941 *They Were Strong and Good* by Robert Lawson (Viking Kestrel)

1940 *Abraham Lincoln* by Ingri and Edgar Parin d'Aulaire (Doubleday)

1939 *Mei Li* by Thomas Handforth (Doubleday)

1938 *Animals of the Bible* by Helen Dean Fish, illustrated by Dorothy P. Lathrop (Lippincott)

Sources

Adventuring with Books by Mary Lou White, ed. National Council of Teachers of English, 1981.

Better Homes & Gardens New Baby Book by Edwin Kiester, Jr., and Sally Valente Kiester. New York: Bantam Books, 1984.

The Early Childhood Years by Frank and Theresa Caplan. New York: Perigee, 1983.

The First Three Years of Life by Burton L. White. New York: Avon Books, 1975.

The First Twelve Months of Life by Frank Caplan. New York: Bantam Books, 1981.

How to Father by Dr. Fitzhugh Dodson. New York: New American Library, 1974.

Ready to Read: A Parents' Guide by Mary Ann Dzama and Robert Gilstrap. New York: John Wiley & Sons, 1983.

The Second Twelve Months of Life by Frank and Theresa Caplan. New York: Perigee, 1977.

Your Baby and Child by Penelope Leach. New York: Knopf, 1983.

Your Baby's Mind and How It Grows: Piaget's Theory for Parents by Mary Ann Spencer Pulaski. New York: Harper Colophon Books, 1978.

Your Five Year Old by Louise Bates Ames and Frances L. Ilg. New York: Dell, 1979.

Your Four Year Old by Louise Bates Ames and Frances L. Ilg. New York: Dell, 1976.

Your Three Year Old by Louise Bates Ames and Frances L. Ilg. New York: Dell, 1976.

Your Two Year Old by Louise Bates Ames and Frances L. Ilg. New York: Dell, 1976.

Title Index

Author Index

Illustrator Index

Adams, Adrienne, 95, 105
Ahlberg, Allan, 26–27, 44
Ahlberg, Janet, 26–27, 44
Alexander, Martha, 58, 87
Aliki, 95–96
Angeli, Marguerite de, 14
Anno, Mitsumasa, 24
Ardizzone, Edward, 98–99
Aruego, Jose, 63, 70–71
Asch, Frank, 62
Atkinson, Allen, 15, 16–17

Baird, Anne, 32
Bang, Molly, 69
Barret, Ron, 94–95
Barton, Byron, 45, 77
Baskin, Leonard, 12
Bemelmans, Ludwig, 63–64
Berenstain, Jan, 41
Berenstain, Stan, 41
Bishop, Claire Huchet, 96
Blegvad, Erik, 103
Blum, Rochelle, 43
Boon, Emilie, 66
Boynton, Sandra, 32

Bracken, Carolyn, 43, 52
Brett, Jan, 43
Briggs, Raymond, 16, 68
Bright, Robert, 81, 86
Brown, Marc, 26
Brown, Margaret Wise, 42–43
Bruna, Dick, 47, 60, 61
Brunhoff, Jean de, 19
Burningham, John, 46, 61–62, 63, 65, 78
Burton, Virginia Lee, 63, 85
Butler, John, 82–83

Campbell, Rod, 32–33, 35, 42
Carle, Eric, 35–36, 41–42, 70
Cashman, Doug, 37
Chalmers, Mary, 87
Chauhan, Manhar, 26
Chorao, Kay, 46
Cooney, Barbara, 58, 67
Cosgrove, Stephen, 68
Craig, Helen, 46
Crews, Donald, 58–59
Cummings, Pat, 98